THE
3-DEGREE
PUTTING SOLUTION

THE
3-DEGREE
PUTTING SOLUTION

THE COMPREHENSIVE, SCIENTIFICALLY PROVEN GUIDE TO BETTER PUTTING

MICHAEL BREED **with**
JOHN STEINBREDER

GOTHAM
BOOKS

GOTHAM BOOKS
Published by Penguin Group (USA) Inc.
375 Hudson Street, New York, New York 10014, U.S.A.
Penguin Group (Canada), 90 Eglinton Avenue East, Suite 700, Toronto, Ontario M4P 2Y3,
Canada (a division of Pearson Penguin Canada Inc.); Penguin Books Ltd, 80 Strand, London
WC2R 0RL, England; Penguin Ireland, 25 St Stephen's Green, Dublin 2, Ireland (a division of
Penguin Books Ltd); Penguin Group (Australia), 250 Camberwell Road, Camberwell, Victoria
3124, Australia (a division of Pearson Australia Group Pty Ltd); Penguin Books India Pvt Ltd,
11 Community Centre, Panchsheel Park, New Delhi – 110 017, India; Penguin Group (NZ), 67
Apollo Drive, Rosedale, Auckland 0632, New Zealand (a division of Pearson New Zealand
Ltd); Penguin Books (South Africa) (Pty) Ltd, 24 Sturdee Avenue, Rosebank, Johannesburg
2196, South Africa

Penguin Books Ltd, Registered Offices: 80 Strand, London WC2R 0RL, England

Published by Gotham Books, a member of Penguin Group (USA) Inc.

First printing, October 2011

10 9 8 7 6 5 4 3 2 1
Copyright © 2011 by Michael Breed

LIBRARY OF CONGRESS CATALOGING-IN-PUBLICATION DATA
Breed, Michael.
The 3-degree putting solution : the comprehensive, scientifically proven guide to better
putting / by Michael Breed with John Steinbreder.
   p. cm.
   ISBN 978-1-59240-656-2 (hardback)
   1. Putting (Golf)—Handbooks, manuals, etc. 2. Golf—Training—Handbooks, manuals,
etc. I. Steinbreder, John. II. Title. III. Title: Three-degree putting solution.
GV979.P8B74 2011
796.352'35—dc22   2011016441

Printed in the United States of America

Set in Garth Graphic
Designed by Sabrina Bowers

While the author has made every effort to provide accurate telephone numbers and Internet
addresses at the time of publication, neither the publisher nor the author assumes any
responsibility for errors, or for changes that occur after publication. Further, the publisher
does not have any control over and does not assume any responsibility for author or
third-party websites or their content.

To my wife, Kerri. Your love, trust, honesty, humor, patience, support, beauty, intelligence, and character are more than I dreamed possible. You are the blessing of my life. The wait was so worth it. I love you.

CONTENTS

INTRODUCTION WHAT I FOUND IN THE MORNING DEW   I

CHAPTER ONE GET A GRIP (AND GET POSITION AND ALIGNMENT RIGHT, TOO)   II

CHAPTER TWO THE STROKE   21

CHAPTER THREE BE NEGATIVE—WITH YOUR PUTTER LOFT   33

CHAPTER FOUR SPEED, ROLL, AND FORWARD AXIS OF ROTATION   43

CHAPTER FIVE READING THE GREENS   49

CHAPTER SIX BE POSITIVE—WITH YOUR MENTAL APPROACH   57

CHAPTER SEVEN GOOD-BYE, MR. YIPS   71

CHAPTER EIGHT CUSTOMIZATION, AND THE BEST PUTTER FOR YOU   81

CHAPTER NINE USING THE VIDEO CAMERA   93

CHAPTER TEN DRILLS, GAMES, AND PRACTICE   105

ACKNOWLEDGMENTS   147

INTRODUCTION

What I Found in the Morning Dew

THE IDEA FIRST CAME TO ME NEARLY THIRTY YEARS AGO, WHEN I was practicing early one morning before a round of golf with my father. I was putting golf balls across a dew-covered green and could clearly see the line of each Titleist as it cut through the thin film of water covering the closely cropped grass. The ball always jumped into the air immediately after impact with my putter face, landing on the ground a few inches from where it had been resting and leaving a mark in the dew. It bounced a few times, and only then did it actually start rolling.

I was curious about that, as I had never understood why a ball hopped off a putterface. I figured it might have been because most off-the-rack putters, including the one I was using at the time, had a couple of degrees of loft built into them, and that loft forced the ball into the air. Then I thought I might be doing something wrong when I stroked the ball. So I started toying with shaft positions to see what sorts of changes I could make to the way the ball reacted when I hit it.

That's how I usually am when I practice. I'm curious. I like to tinker. I notice things like the sound a ball makes when it comes off the clubface and the shape of a divot after a shot. I'm always interested in ways I can improve my game and help those around me, too. I love figuring things out.

Fiddling with my putter that day, I quickly realized that by leaning the shaft forward, I was able to transform the loft from positive to negative. In the process, I all but eliminated that jump in the ball, and it began to roll more consistently to the cup with topspin—and not check up with backspin the way it did when it landed after that initial hop. The ball didn't slow down so quickly, or die so suddenly to the short side of the cup, and I found myself stroking each putt with a pure roll.

My first reaction was: "This is very cool!" My second reaction was: "I think I've discovered something pretty significant."

Actually, "rediscovered" is a better word, because what I had stumbled upon was a truth that the great putters of yesteryear had known: A golfer creates forward rotation when he hits his putts with negative loft. The result of that forward rotation is consistent speed and ball direction, which allows players to be more effective putters. That's what Billy Casper, Horton Smith, and Bobby Locke did as they putted their ways into the World Golf Hall of Fame. It's also the method Dave Stockton used to win two PGA Championships, and to earn the praise of his fellow pros as one of the best flatstick players (and teachers) of all time. In fact, Walter Travis, who won the U.S. Amateur in 1900 and the British Amateur four years later, had similar ideas. Travis was a superb short-game artist who famously gave Bobby Jones a lesson that the golfing great credited with making him a better putter. And the center-shafted, mallet-headed Schenectady putter Travis used to win so many of his championships remains one of the most famous clubs golf has ever known. He also published a much praised book in 1901, *Practical Golf*, espousing several theories on putting. Including this one: "So it is with a straight-faced putter as against one a trifle lofted or laid back. The more it [a putter face] is laid back, the greater is the undercut or backward spin and the harder must the ball be struck."

The problem was, most modern golf instructors had long ago forgotten that truth about negative loft, and it had been years since anyone had actively promoted or taught the concept. Instead, they advocated positive loft, among other alternative putting theories.

As for me, I didn't even think about Casper and Locke or Stockton and Smith that day on the practice green when I first moved my hands forward and leaned my puttershaft toward the cup to see if I could get the ball to jump a little less—and roll a little more. I was young. I had no idea the direction I would take in this great game of golf. I didn't know that I would become a well-respected teaching professional. I was simply trying to make sense of something I did not understand.

And the more I worked with that approach, the more I saw the benefits. It was hard to hold back a happy, satisfied grin.

Ben Hogan famously said he uncovered his secrets of the game in the dirt of the practice tee. I had found mine in the morning dew, although it would be more than twenty years before I could truly verify those discoveries.

To better understand how and why the golf ball reacted differently to negative loft, I thought of the behavior of a cue ball in pool. If a player wants to create backspin and cause the ball to stop suddenly, the contact point with the cue stick is the lower half of the ball, below the equator. If, however, he wants to create forward rotation so the ball rolls directly to the hole, the contact point must be the upper half.

The only way to reach a contact point on the lower half of a golf ball is with a putter that has positive loft—i.e., one in which the clubface slants slightly back from the bottom to the top, the same way the face of a driver or 5-iron does, only much less so. The greater the loft, the lower the impact point. To create forward rotation, and hit the golf ball above the equator, a player needs to have his putter in a forward position when he makes contact. He has to create that negative loft, in which the upper part of the putter hits the upper part of the ball and creates a higher impact point.

On that morning when I first noticed the way in which the golf ball rolled, I was in college, playing competitively for the golf team at Randolph-Macon College, a small, Division III school in Ashland, Virginia. I thought seriously about playing for a living after I graduated from there in 1985 with a degree in psychology. I entered some mini-tour events in Florida and New England, but it didn't take long to realize that while I was a good player, I was not PGA Tour caliber. So I began to teach, first as an assistant pro at the Dorset Field Club in Dorset, Vermont, and then at the Birchwood Golf Club in Westport, Connecticut. And it was at those jobs that I started to think long and hard about the putting stroke—and started to formulate the theories that I'm advancing in this book.

My interest in putting actually started when I looked at my own game when I was competing and thought about the ways I could get better. Better ballstriking was one, of course. And putting another. So I started keeping track of my putts—which ones I made, which ones I missed, and why. Then my research moved into my work as an instructor, where I saw the different ways my students struggled with their putting and what tweaks and fixes helped improve their performances. And it wasn't long before I expanded my studies beyond the practice green and started examining the techniques of the game's best putters in books, magazines, and on video. That's when I found that so many of them had created negative loft, either by leaning their clubshaft forward slightly (which is what the great Mickey Wright did), or by "hooding" the face (which was Horton Smith's style). That's when I knew I was onto something.

However, I also knew I had much more work to do in order to counter the new conventional wisdom. This was the late 1980s, when a technology revolution was shaking up golf and the greatest equipment advances in the history of the game were coming onstream. Many equipment makers were using high-speed cameras to study the putting stroke and how golf balls reacted when they were struck. One of the pivotal "insights" from that time was the observation that the weight of a golf ball sitting motionless on a green created a slight "depression" in the turf. The ball, they pointed out, was nestled in an almost imperceptible "cup." As a result, manufacturers and designers decided that putters needed to have a loft of about 3 or 4 degrees so that golfers could "lift" or "pop" their golf ball out of this depression and send it toward the hole. Golf instructors soon began buying into that argument, and as a result, they began seeing positive loft as the solution to a newly discovered problem.

But the deeper I dug into the subject, the more skeptical I became of that thinking.

I knew that forward lean and negative loft worked. My own experimentation on the putting green told me that, and so did the videos and photographs I studied of players like Casper, Smith, Locke, and Wright. Pretty soon I was teaching the benefits of negative loft to my students, some of whom were competing on the professional golf tours. It was the start of what became a sort of doctoral study of the putting stroke.

It was around this time that I decided to focus on becoming a putting teacher. I wanted to make it my specialty, the thing that drew students to me. A lot of instructors taught the golf swing. But no one was really paying attention at the time to the putting stroke. That made me believe that I could make a difference in the game if I concentrated on putting instruction. I was certain that if I helped players putt better, they would improve. I knew from my own experience that the more putts I made, the lower scores I shot.

Fewer putts equal lower scores. What a revelation! And I figured that out all by myself!

I also knew I was onto something unique with that idea of negative loft. I could see the results in the way I putted as a competitor on mini-tour and sectional golf events. And as an assistant professional at the Augusta National Golf Club, where I worked from 1990 to 1992, and later as an assistant at the Deepdale Golf Club on Long Island, I watched my negative-loft method help my students improve as well. Before long, I noticed I was getting busier and busier as an instructor, and that my students had begun to include club professionals from my PGA section. Even my boss at Deepdale, the noted player and teacher Darrell Kestner, started working with me. My teaching schedule became even more hectic when I took the head professional's job at Sunningdale Country Club in Scarsdale, New York, in the spring of 2001, and people really began paying attention to my theories on putting. But I didn't have any proof, and I knew I needed proof to show that what I was teaching was indeed correct.

So I started to do even more research. I spent hundreds of hours studying the concept with video recorders, swing monitors, and digital cameras. I began to analyze the putting stroke from every possible angle. I started to examine what the ball, body, and hands were doing during the putt itself. I thought it made sense to consider what was going on in a golfer's head when he was trying to drain a five-footer, and so I also sat down with top touring pros like Ben Crenshaw, Loren Roberts, and Brad Faxon and kicked around ideas on putting and the forward-lean theories I had. I spent hours with some of the best teaching and playing club professionals in the country, too, bouncing thoughts off them. At the same time, I began amassing an extensive library of putting books, both old and new, featuring the thoughts of players as diverse as Willie Park Jr. and Crenshaw, as well as Locke and Smith. I wanted to learn all the little secrets as I delved even more deeply into the one I had found. The one about forward roll and negative loft.

I discovered a lot in my studies. I learned, for example, that Park, the two-time British Open champion and celebrated short-game artist, had advocated forward shaft lean in a book he wrote in 1920, and that

Horton Smith had described the benefits of imparting forward spin to his putts in a 1961 volume.

At this point, I could not get my hands on enough putting books. I also continued to carefully consider what the ball did every time it came off the putterface when I was playing, practicing, or teaching. I noticed it always jumped into the air when it was struck with loft, and the more I looked at that, the more I thought of what I had discovered in the dew that morning on the putting green—and the more I understood what was going on.

As I was doing this, I realized I was becoming a really good putter, and many times I felt I could make everything I looked at. My pace and control of putts at places like Augusta National and Deepdale, which are famous for greens that are very true, very fast, and full of undulations, felt unbelievable. I remember shooting 65 and 66 in successive rounds one weekend at Augusta and appreciating afterward that my speed was perfect both those days, even on the putts I didn't make.

At the same time, my reputation as a teacher was growing. The Metropolitan Section of the PGA of America named me Teacher of the Year in 2000. Two years later, a student of mine, Chris Smith, won a PGA Tour event at Westchester Country Club outside New York just after we had spent a day working on his putting. In 2003, *Golf Magazine* selected me as one of the Top 100 instructors in the country, and six years later, the Met PGA honored me as its Teacher of the Year again. Interestingly, I also received the Horton Smith Award from that same section twice in 2007 and 2008 for outstanding and continuing contributions to professional education. And in 2010, I accepted the Ely Callaway Award from the Met PGA for member service and self-improvement achievements. I was also one of four finalists for the PGA of America's National Teacher of the Year honor.

Pretty good stuff, to be sure. And I was totally committed to my theories of negative loft and the importance of forward shaft lean and the good roll it imparted. I had faith in what I was doing, and I had been teaching the concept of forward roll and negative loft for nearly twenty years with great success. But I still had no proof. So, I commissioned a firm in Dallas, Texas, to conduct a series of tests for me so that I could finally receive absolute confirmation of my system.

For those tests, the firm employed a device called the "Green Machine" that grips a putter and then produces a consistent stroke, much like the "Iron Byron" machine the United States Golf Association uses to test golf clubs and balls at its headquarters in Far Hills, New Jersey. The device was calibrated to ensure that it struck a golf ball with sufficient force to produce a putt of 26 feet using a club with the 3 degrees of positive loft that is standard issue for most commercial putters. Then it used that same stroke to hit putters with varying degrees of clubface loft. What the testing firm discovered was that the greater the loft in a putter, the shorter the distance the putt hit with the same stroke traveled, while a putt hit with negative loft went significantly farther because it had forward rotation.

I'll get into the specifics of what the testing revealed later in this book. But generally speaking, it demonstrated that the sooner you can put forward spin on the ball, the more consistent your speed and distance will be. That's because to roll the ball the same distance, you have to make a bigger stroke with a putter having 3 or 4 degrees of positive loft than one with -3 degrees. And the bigger the stroke you have to make, the more errors you can introduce into the stroke itself and the less consistent your stroke will be. As any golfer facing a testy approach shot with a wedge or short iron knows, it's easier to make good contact with the ball with a shortened stroke. It's the same with putting: It's easier to hit the ball with the center of the clubface when you're making a less exaggerated stroke. Further, you will have to hit the ball harder with a longer putt, and that will make the ball jump farther into the air.

Why do all this testing, which cost me thousands of dollars? Why pour all that money and time into it? Because I was out there saying the world was round with my beliefs in negative loft, while everyone else was saying it was flat. Though I was considered one of the better teachers in the country, I couldn't get anyone in the industry other than my students to buy wholeheartedly into my ideas. And I was determined to get proof one way or another. When I did, when I received those results from Dallas, it was like finding the proverbial pot of gold. I was beyond excited.

That's because the results demonstrated what I had long thought to be true: The reverse rotation initiated when a golfer employs a lofted putter actually takes away his control of the ball. And once a golfer loses control of speed and direction, he is far less likely to produce an accurate and successful putt.

To be sure, a ball hit with negative loft *may* still jump up from the depression in which it rests on the green, just not as high or as far as one hit with positive loft. As a result, it will roll with more consistent speed and rotation, enabling golfers to retain more control of how far and fast their putts run. That consistency and control will not only help them make more putts, it will also stave off cases of the dreaded "yips," which occur when players become so uncertain as to how hard they should hit a putt that they begin flinching when they get ready to make a stroke (I'll talk about this later, in Chapter Seven).

The secret was in the loft. The solution, too. Three degrees of negative loft. The 3-Degree Putting Solution. Its simplicity did not diminish its significance. I felt that I had discovered the cure to the most debilitating, unnerving, depressing, and score-shredding disease in golf: the malignancy known as bad putting.

Having validated my theories, I now want to share them with as many golfers as possible. I also want to show those golfers how they can become much more proficient at putting by creating negative loft when they putt and imparting forward rotation on the golf ball. As I deal with keys to green reading and mental conditioning, I want to provide groundbreaking information on grip, posture, and alignment, as well as club path, face angle, and tempo. In addition, I want to offer them a series of drills, games, and practice tips designed to reinforce my teachings and enhance putting prowess, along with a section on how they can use video equipment as simple as their cell phones to help them in their quest to become a better putter.

Now, some might wonder why I want to devote an entire book to putting; or why I spent the better part of twenty years researching and analyzing every intricacy of that part of the game and invested thousands of dollars to prove my points. After all, the rules of golf allow a player to carry fourteen clubs in his bag, which means that the putter is only one of many weapons in a golfer's arsenal.

But the fact is, the putter is the most important club in the bag. On average, putts account for 43 percent of all strokes in an 18-hole round. Great putting is what separates a great player from someone who is merely good enough to compete on the fringe of the PGA Tour. The best players on the top tours are not the longest hitters, although some of those certainly do well. They are the best putters. Jack Nicklaus won those eighteen professional majors because he knew how to get the ball into the hole. He knew how to putt. Tiger Woods was celebrated for his prodigious length off the tee when he first joined the PGA Tour, and he is frequently lauded for the tremendous recovery shots he hits around trees and over hazards as well as for his remarkable accuracy with approach shots. But putting is the part of his game that has contributed the most to his success.

Great putting is what wins tournaments at the pro level, and if you aren't so sure about that, consider that the player who led the field in driving distance in each PGA Tour event in 2009 ended up winning only once: Dustin Johnson, at the AT&T National Pro-Am at Pebble Beach. But the fellow who had the lowest number of putts in a round won six times. It also makes sense to look at 2010 and one Matt Kuchar. The week of the season-ending Tour Championship the cheerful Georgian was not only number 1 in FedEx Cup points but also first on the PGA Tour money list. His rank in putting? Twentieth. In driving distance, he stood 104th.

Another case worth analyzing is that of Steve Stricker, ranked 4th in the world at that same time in 2010, and 4th on both the FedEx Cup points and PGA Tour money lists. Though his driving puts him 132nd among PGA Tour pros, his putting has him at number 12.

The simple fact is: Putting wins. It wins on the pro tours, it wins at the elite amateur competitions, and it wins member-guests and Saturday morning Nassaus at clubs and public-access courses. And when you become a better putter, you become a better golfer.

You can boom all your drives. You can hit your hybrids tight and your irons stiff. You can cover flags with your wedges. But you cannot go low if you can't putt, and golf is most definitely a game designed to eliminate strokes with the putter. It's amazing how some of my best students—low-handicap golfers with elegant swings and admirable ballstriking skills—kinda sorta know this but don't fully accept it. I recall a typical example from last year. One of the Sunningdale members came into the pro shop after finishing a round. When I asked how he did, he proudly held up his scorecard and said, "I shot a 78. With four three-putts." The meaning behind that statement was hard to miss. He was telling me that he had a great day of ballstriking from tee to green. He striped the ball down the fairways and nailed his approach shots. If he had only putted better—that is, if he had two-putted instead of three-putting on those holes and made a few others—he might have shot around par. That's a lot of what-ifs in a round of golf. The cold, hard fact was that he shot 78, not 71. But in separating his bad putting from the rest of his game, he was minimizing the importance of putting. Worse, he was actually excusing it—and practically ensuring that three-putts would continue to be an integral part of his game, regardless of how well he struck the ball off the tee or the fairway.

Golf, however, is not about the perfection of the full swing. It's about getting the ball into the hole in the fewest strokes possible—and efficient, accurate putting is the surest way to lower the stroke count.

Unfortunately, most golfers don't understand how critical the putter is. I know guys who spend $1,000 on a set of custom-fitted irons, and more than a few hours getting properly fitted for them, but then think nothing of grabbing any old putter out of the pro shop and jamming it into their bag. They don't understand the need to treat that element of the game with the same time and consideration that they give to their driving. They don't realize that they can derive as much tactile pleasure—perhaps more—from a well-struck putt on the practice green as they get from nailing their drivers and irons on the range.

In this book, I will show you how to find your putting stroke and help you understand why the "perfect" putts you hit all the time are not going in. There is logic to putting well, and science behind the success. There is a solution, too. The 3-Degree Putting Solution.

Now, let's do it!

CHAPTER ONE

GET A GRIP

(And Get Position and Alignment Right, Too)

GRIPPING A GOLF CLUB IS NOT ONLY THE FIRST THING YOU DO when you set out to play a round, it's also the most important, because it's your only connection to the golf club. And it's been that way since Scotsman H. B. Farnie wrote the first golf instruction book back in 1857. Even then, golf teachers talked about how critical it was to grip the club properly, and nothing about that philosophy has changed in all that time. In fact, grip is as significant a consideration today as it has ever been, particularly when it comes to putting. Or, should I say, most especially when it comes to putting.

Grip is the predictor of posture, balance, and putter flow. Certain things happen to your body, and ultimately your stroke, when you hold the putter in certain ways. So before we talk about anything else in putting, we must discuss the grip.

As far as I'm concerned, there is only one way to properly hold the putter, and that is in the palms of your hands, not in your fingers. I don't care whether you prefer a conventional grip or lead-hand low. What I am concerned about, however, is that your contact with the club comes through your palms.

In fact, I am so concerned about the grip that I worked with the good people at Golf Pride to develop the Life Line grip. It is an instructional grip with molded placements for the proper positioning of your hands so that you hold the putter properly. In the palms.

Why do I worry so much about the grip? More than twenty years of intently studying the putting stroke has shown me that most problems occur when golfers hold their putters in their fingers. That's because you have much more agility when you grip a golf club that way. That agility leads to wrist movement, and wrist movement is a killer. When you break your wrists, you change the loft of your putter as well as the impact point between the clubface and the ball. And if you do not have those 3 degrees of negative loft at impact and are not making contact with the ball at or slightly above the equator, you are not going to be able to impart the optimum forward roll in the ball— and you won't be able to produce the consistent speed you want on the greens. As a result, you won't be able to make nearly as many putts.

Breaking your wrists also causes you to open and close the putterface. That affects direction, because it forces you to either pull or push the ball. And you cannot hole putts with any sort of regularity if you're doing that.

But when you hold your putter in the palms of your hands, you lessen wrist movement, eliminate face rotation, and are able to produce consistent speed and direction more easily.

Consistency in the putting stroke is key, because inconsistent putting is what vexes most golfers. You know the syndrome. You putt like a touring pro on one hole, and like you've never played the game before on the next five. Golfers far too often blame such spates of bad fortune on the Putting Gods, suddenly acting as though they live in ancient times and ascribing the reason for every good and bad thing in their lives to some mercurial deity. But more often than not, their failure with the flatstick is the result of an inconsistent putting stroke. And that inconsistency stems from the use of an improper grip.

TO CREATE THE PROPER GRIP, YOU MUST HOLD YOUR PUTTER IN THE palms of your hand, with the grip set in the crease that's formed when you squeeze your heel pad and thumb pad together. Your fingers should press against the grip instead of wrapping around it, and the top of the grip should point up your lead arm. It may feel like you're arching your lead wrist a bit, but that's good for stability.

I LIKE A GOLFER'S FOREARMS TO BE ON THE SAME PLANE AS HIS PUTTER-shaft. You can't do that when you hold the club in your fingers, as you would an iron. But when you put the putter in your palms, with the shaft running on a straight line from your elbows through the putter-head, you'll have the putter held properly. Your body will move as one, instead of as many moving parts, and you'll have a much better chance of making consistent contact at those optimum impact points and of controlling your distance and speed.

Why does this work? For one thing, you can do only so much bending and flexing when you grip your putter that way. Having it in your palms creates that stability. It promotes consistency in the stroke, and it keeps the wrists from breaking down. It keeps the fingers from getting overactive. It allows you to maintain that optimum 3 degrees of negative loft and hit the ball more easily at the proper impact point. That way, you impart the forward spin that is so important to good putting—and you avoid the backspin and sidespin that come from mishits and those that are off target. It can also prevent you from holding your putter too tightly, which is never a good thing.

I am unyielding on this issue of grip, because to putt properly, you have to putt the ball with a high degree of exactness. The game is simply built that way. We start from hitting a drive off the tee to a fairway some 30 yards wide. Then, if we're playing a par-4, we hit our second shots onto a green that is also pretty big—perhaps 5,000 to 7,000 square feet in size. But from there, we have to putt our golf ball into a cup that is 4¼ inches in diameter. All of a sudden, we're forced to get much more exact.

As a rule, the full swings we take with our drivers and fairway metals, hybrids, and irons are directional. We pretty much know how far we hit them because the clubs have already been calibrated for distance based on your clubhead speed and the loft of your club. We just need to hit them in the right direction.

But putting is different, because we have to consider direction *and* distance. You don't have one putter for 50-foot putts and another for five-footers the way you have a 9-iron that goes, say, 130 yards and a 6-iron that you hit 170. You have to take care of both those yourself, which is why you have to be so exact. And the best way to ensure that exactness—exactness that will lead to a good, consistent stroke—is to hold the putter in your palms.

AS FOR THE OPTIMUM CLUB POSITION AT ADDRESS, I LIKE IT WHEN THE sole of the putter is flat on the ground and the shaft is leaning forward slightly, so that the handle of the putter is closer to the target than the clubhead. That creates the desired negative loft and enables you to put the proper forward rotation on the ball.

MY STUDENTS ASK ME ABOUT POSTURE ALL THE TIME, AND HERE'S MY take on the subject: Your elbows can have some bend, and there should be bend in your waist, as well as some slight knee flex. I think it's good to have about 60 percent of your weight on your forward leg. I also prefer the shoulders to be square (parallel to the target line) or slightly open (to the target line). I don't want them closed, because that makes it hard to look down the target line. And when I look at the target, I want my eyes to do so with my head more upright, with my eyes parallel to the ground instead of perpendicular. Your shoulders shouldn't be rounded either—that can cause you to bend too much in the spine, and it will keep your body from moving as freely as it should. That can lock your body down and cause you to get too wristy.

I'm a big believer in keeping the eyes on or inside the ball line. That allows you to look at the putt with your eyes in their normal position—that is, parallel to the ground rather than perpendicular. This also allows you to see the target as you normally see, and will help you achieve a better and more consistent line and stroke.

I CAUTION MY STUDENTS ALL THE TIME ABOUT STANDING TOO FAR OVER the ball, and I quickly suggest a drill if it seems that they're making a habit of that. If they're right-handed, I have them hold a golf ball just below their right eye when they set up (or just below their left eye if they're left-handed), and then ask them to drop the ball. If it falls by the hosel of the club, their setup is fine. If the ball lands well inside the putterhead, they need to get closer to the ball.

This is a great drill, and one that should be performed regularly. (For more drills related to grip, position, and alignment—and other critical aspects of putting—check out Chapter Nine.)

When it comes to clubface alignment, I like to have the center of the putter aimed toward the target—and to be on that line at impact. Remember, I'm talking about the target here, not necessarily the hole. If you want to hit your putt to the left edge of the cup, for example, you want the impact point and face aligned to that target, and the center of the putterface moving down the line, too.

Ball position is another very important matter and can vary from player to player. The key is to do what you must to get enough shaft lean to transform a putter that has, say, two degrees of positive loft into one with the optimum three degrees of negative loft, in order to achieve that preferred forward roll. There are different ways to do that, whether it's through shaft lean or stance width or weight distribution, and I'll get into those later on in the book. Just remember that how you get that negative loft is not as important as whether you get it at all.

There has been so much discussion among top golf instructors over the years about ball position as it relates to a golfer's feet, but to me it's an upper-body thing. I care about where the ball is in relation to your upper spine. And I want the ball absolutely in line with your upper spine. Why? Because your hands come together at your spine, and when you hold the putter that way, you'll see that for a right-handed golfer, the head on the vast majority of putters is just right of center, due to its offset.

ALIGNING THE BALL WITH YOUR UPPER SPINE IS THE PROPER WAY TO know where your ball should be at all times. We can't always be sure that we're spacing our feet the same distance putt after putt after putt, and this makes it very hard to know whether we're playing the ball off the same spot all the time. But the position of our spine never changes.

As we wrap up this first chapter, remember that my goal is to put you in the position to become the most successful and consistent putter possible. And I need to start that process by making sure that your grip, position, and alignment are right. It's like getting ready for a big road trip. You have to have all the essentials organized before you begin to drive. Gas in the car. Air in the tires. Good music ready to play. And directions.

Keep in mind that what you do before you move the putter, what I call pre-swing, is vitally important. Make sure your fundamentals with regard to grip, position, and alignment are correct before you make your stroke. If you're flawed pre-swing, you can be assured that your putting stroke will be flawed as well.

CHAPTER TWO

THE STROKE

GOLFERS HAVE EMPLOYED A VARIETY OF PUTTING TECHNIQUES over the years. Part of that has always been a matter of what equipment was available, and also where they were playing. Old Tom Morris banged gutta perchas with a wooden, long-nosed putter on the scrubby links of St. Andrews in the late 1880s with a much different stroke from the one Ben Crenshaw used with his sleek, steel-headed Wilson 8802 when he won the Masters on a verdant and pristine Augusta National course a century later. Style has often factored into the equation, too, with players of the same eras putting on similar types of courses in very dissimilar ways.

Putting strokes are unique in that regard. While every other part of the golf swing has been analyzed for centuries, very little attention has been paid to the science of putting until fairly recently. Rather than breaking down the way men and women putted, golfers mostly talked about the individualistic nature of the strokes they used on the greens. That's one reason why putting lessons have only become semi-popular in the last twenty years or so. It was never on the menu before then. Putting, and putting strokes, were afterthoughts.

Thankfully, we are now examining this subject with much greater clarity, interest, and depth. And the result can only be lower scores and lower handicaps for golfers who are willing to take the time to understand and appreciate how important a proper putting stroke is—and to learn the best ways to execute one.

Golfers like you, who are taking the time to read this book.

A PROPER PUTTING STROKE IS A FLUID MOTION ENERGIZED BY THE BIG muscles in your shoulders and upper back, not your hands and wrists. To start your stroke, your lead shoulder (the left one for a right-handed player) should go down slightly as you bring the putter back. Then the back shoulder should go down as you begin to go through the ball. It's like a seesaw in that sense, and you want your lower back and trunk stable when you make your stroke. As I've mentioned before, you must keep your hands and wrists quiet throughout the process. If they get overactive, you will inadvertently change the loft of your putter as well as the alignment of the clubface. And there is no way you can be consistent with your distance and direction—and your overall putting—if you can't be consistent with your loft (negative three degrees) and face alignment (square at impact).

So you need to develop a putting stroke that eliminates the possibility of those problems occurring, that gets the upper back and shoulders engaged as it keeps the hands and wrists quiet.

Earlier in this chapter, I mentioned that putting has long had a very personal and individualistic nature. But for all the different ways that golfers have putted over the years and the different styles they've used, there are really only three basic putting strokes, and they can all be effective:

1. Straight-back/Straight-through
2. Arc-back/Arc-through
3. Arc-back/Straight-through

SOME PLAYERS LIKE THE ARC-BACK/ARC-THROUGH BECAUSE IT USES A path very similar to the one they employ in their regular golf swings: The putterhead goes inside, then out, and then back in, with the face opening and closing slightly in the backswing and follow-through, but remaining "square" to the path of the arc and square to the target line at impact. Two of the best putters of the modern era, Tiger Woods and Brad Faxon, favor that approach, as does Ben Crenshaw. The path moves in an arc, with the putterface staying square to that arc and the putter-head relatively close to the ground as it moves both back and through.

OTHER GOLFERS OPT FOR A COMBINATION STROKE, THE ARC-BACK/ straight-through, in which they bring the putter back slightly to the inside in the backstroke but then keep the putterhead moving straight down the target line once they've made contact with the ball. That's the method that Horton Smith preferred—he took the putterhead slightly inside and then made sure he struck the ball with a square clubface that stayed square through the follow-through. Bobby Locke putted this way, too. Both golfers said they "hooded" their putters when they did that—they didn't feel that the clubface should be open in any way when they made contact with the ball. In fact, they thought it should remain square to the target line throughout. And they rotated the knuckles in their left hand counterclockwise in their stroke to make sure that happened.

FINALLY, THERE IS THE STRAIGHT-BACK/STRAIGHT-THROUGH METHOD, which is pretty much what it sounds like. The path of the putterhead is always on the target line with this type of stroke, and the face maintains a square relationship to that line all the way back and through the ball. The putterhead moves off the ground quite a bit more than it does with an arc stroke, because in order to stay on the target line, it must move up in the air on both the backstroke and after it moves through the ball.

Loren Roberts putts that way, and the great Jack Nicklaus was a straight-back/straight-through guy more than anything else. He made all those important putts, and won all those big tournaments, using that stroke.

Now, I'm not crazy enough to compare my stroke with Jack's. But straight-back/straight-through is how I putt, and that's what I recommend for my students. In my view, you have the most consistent and powerful transference of energy from backswing, to impact with the ball, to follow-through when you take the putter straight back and then straight through. And if you have a hard time comprehending that, think of a car colliding with a tree: A head-on collision is going to be much more powerful than one that comes from any sort of angle. It's that way in golf, too.

If the putter starts to come off the target line, as it would if you used the arc-back/arc-through or the arc-back/straight-through strokes, you can re-rotate the putterhead. That can cause the transference of energy to decrease, and the impact points to change, which can lead to dreaded inconsistencies in distance.

Once you affect energy transfer, you affect the speed of the putt. And whenever that happens, your ability to be consistent is compromised.

Let me be clear: I am not opposed to using strokes other than straight-back/straight-through. But if you're going to employ either of them, be sure to make that complete transference of energy with each and every putt.

Whatever you decide, the key is to utilize the stroke that gives you the optimum tempo and fluidity. Those attributes are what separate the finest PGA Tour putters of the modern era, like Faxon, Crenshaw, and Woods, from all the others, and you can see it in the remarkably calm and effective way in which they wield their flatsticks. Developing a stroke that has both attributes—tempo and fluidity—will go a long way toward making you a great putter.

Tempo frequently varies from golfer to golfer, and that's fine. The key is to make sure that your tempo has a consistent rhythm to the stroke, a tempo in which the speed of the putter as it goes back and then comes through the ball remains constant. That way, you're making yours a putting "stroke," rather than a putting "hit."

It's also critical that you keep your club going through the ball when you putt, instead of stopping your stroke as soon as you make contact. That kind of deceleration is especially common on fast greens, when a recreational player can get a bit anxious about hitting his putt way past the hole. The blade of the putter will often open up, causing the player to cut across the ball. That, of course, greatly impairs both speed and line.

ONE WAY TO PRODUCE A GOOD, CONSISTENT TEMPO—AND TO ENSURE that you don't decelerate—is to be very precise with the length of your stroke. I prefer a ratio between backswing and follow-through of about one to one and a half. In other words, if your backswing goes back one foot, your follow-through should go one and a half feet. That's because the putterhead should have more speed coming through the ball than going back. That way you'll avoid deceleration.

Deceleration has been a problem for even top touring pros. Remember Doug Sanders in the 1970 British Open Championship, missing that downhill three-footer on the 72nd hole to leave him in a tie with Nicklaus? A day later, Sanders, who was called the "Peacock of the Fairways" for the colorful clothes he wore, lost an 18-hole playoff to Jack. A similar thing happened to Scott Hoch at the 1989 Masters, when he missed a two-footer on the first playoff hole, opening the door for Nick Faldo's first green jacket.

Grip pressure can be a factor with tempo, too, and you need to keep yours consistent throughout the putt. If you inadvertently alter that pressure, you can lose the good swing and rhythm of your putt. Your distance control will also suffer because the speed of the putter-head through the hit will not be consistent. And remember, consistent clubhead speed is what we want in a putting stroke.

ONE WAY TO HELP DEAL WITH THAT ISSUE IS TO USE ONE OF MY DRILLS, IN which you take a piece of paper and wrap it around the grip of your putter. Then, grip the club so that you're holding the paper against it, but not so hard that the paper makes noise when you strike the ball. If you grip it too hard, the paper will make noise, as though you were crumpling it up, because a grip that's too tight will cause you to crease the paper that's wrapped around the putter handle.

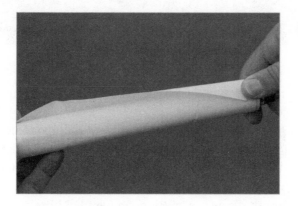

(For more drills to improve your stroke and other matters related to putting, go to Chapter Ten.)

As you have no doubt noticed by now, it is impossible to not talk about speed when we talk about the putting stroke, and I know that by bringing it up here, I'm jumping slightly ahead to Chapter Four. But the matter of speed is that critical. In fact, it may be the most important thing we can discuss in putting. So why hold back?

As golfers, we need to create consistent speed each time we putt. And there are several ways we can do that. One is by ensuring that we always have forward lean on our putter, thus creating negative loft, and that we always hit the ball at a contact point at or above its equator so that we impart topspin and get it rolling with forward rotation. And that jibes nicely with another imperative, which is making a proper putting stroke—one that creates a consistent transference of energy as we go through the ball, and that keeps the hands and wrists quiet as it also maintains consistent tempo.

CHAPTER THREE

BE NEGATIVE—
WITH YOUR PUTTER LOFT

NEGATIVE LOFT IS THE KEY TO GOOD PUTTING, AND I CANNOT emphasize that enough. You must create negative loft with your putter so that you can strike the golf ball at the proper contact point and impart a forward axis of rotation that rolls the ball to the target at a consistent speed.

Negative loft is also one of the most misunderstood and underappreciated scoring techniques in golf—and inarguably one of the most effective.

That's why this chapter merits close reading. Negative loft is a very big deal!

To begin to understand its importance, though, we need to be clear on what negative loft is. And to do that, we must consider loft in general and the face of a putter. There are three types of putter loft: neutral, positive, and negative. If the face is perfectly vertical, perfectly straight from top to bottom, then it's neutral. It has no loft at all. In other words, zero degrees. But if you lean the face back so that your hands are just behind the putter blade and the top of the clubface is slightly behind the bottom, you create positive loft. Doing that makes the putterface look like one of the longer irons in your bag, which are made with positive loft so that it's easier to get a golf ball into the air. Only much less extreme.

IF YOU MOVE YOUR HANDS FORWARD AS YOU GRIP THIS SAME PUTTER, however, you put angle on the face in such a way that the top of the blade is aimed toward the ball, and the entire clubface is angled toward the ground. Golfers call that action "forward lean," and by doing that, you create negative loft. That allows you to hit the ball at or just slightly above its equator in order to get it to roll with a forward axis of rotation.

Now, don't expect to find any putters with zero degrees of loft—let alone any with negative loft—at your club's pro shop or your friendly off-course retailer. That's because the vast majority of commercial putters sold today are made with 3 to 4 degrees of positive loft.

Why positive loft? Because conventional wisdom among most modern clubmakers and teaching professionals says that a golf ball creates a slight "depression" when it sits motionless on a putting green. The ball, the thinking goes, is nestled in an almost imperceptible "cup," and as a result, a golfer needs a putter with positive loft to "lift" that Titleist out of its cups.

Believe it or not, clubmakers used to put even more than three or four degrees of positive loft in their putters. That was back in the old days—the nineteenth century and beyond—when most golfers actually carried two so-called flatsticks in their bags. Generally speaking, one had a few degrees of positive loft for those putts that were stroked exclusively on the greens. But the other putter featured as much as 12 to 15 degrees, because it was designed to hit those long putts of 70 or 80 yards from off the green that are so common on firm and fast links courses. The thinking was that to get those longer putts to the targets, players needed to get their golf ball into the air initially, as modern golfers might when they use a hybrid to hit those shots.

As you well know by now, I do not have a positive view of positive loft at impact, because extensive research and sophisticated testing have demonstrated just how harmful and ineffective it can be to putting. When a golfer hits a putt with positive loft, the lower half of the clubface makes contact with the lower half of the golf ball. That creates backspin, causing the ball to spin initially with reverse rotation and "check up." Then it acquires a second axis of rotation and begins rolling forward, toward the target.

That reverse rotation causes problems. It takes away a player's control of the ball, and once a golfer loses control of speed and direction, he is far less likely to produce an accurate and successful putt.

Hit a putt with negative loft, however, and you all but eliminate that jump in the ball that comes right after impact. It enables you to impart forward rotation and have the putt roll to the target with topspin. It allows you to better control the speed and direction of the ball, and it will not check up with backspin the way it does when it is hit with positive loft. There will be only one axis of rotation, and as a result the ball will roll with consistent speed across the green to the place you have aimed it.

There is nothing very complicated about negative loft. It is easy to understand, and very easy to impart to a golf ball. You do it simply by moving your hands forward so that the clubface is slightly de-lofted and then making contact with the ball at a place at or just above its equator. Do this, and you'll find that you're in much greater control of how far and fast your putts run. Do this, and you'll certainly make more putts than you ever have before. Do this, and you won't get confused about distance anymore.

Hey, I have an idea. Let's do this!

But first, let's take a look at how I got here. As I mentioned in the

Introduction, I first figured out the virtues of negative loft nearly three decades ago, when I was banging putts on that golf club practice green. The marks my Titleists made in the morning dew when they popped off my putterface and landed in the wet grass intrigued me. I never realized they actually jumped so far. I never knew that the ball skidded so much when it landed, or checked up as severely as it did. Then I started fiddling with different shaft positions.

As I did that, I quickly learned that by leaning the shaft forward, I could transform the loft in my putterface from positive to negative, and transform the initial rotation of those golf balls I was stroking from reverse to forward. They were no longer checking up so suddenly. Rather, they started rolling to the target I had selected right away. My putts started to feel more solid, too, and every one I stroked had a pure roll.

I thought I had made a pretty big discovery. But I didn't know whether it might be useful to other golfers. Once I became a teaching pro, however, I started to research the concepts of forward lean and negative loft to see whether it might be applicable to my students. That's when I realized that others had traveled this road well before me—in fact, some pretty significant others. Iconic golf professionals like Willie Park Jr. and Walter Hagen. Billy Casper and Horton Smith. Bobby Locke and Dave Stockton. Negative loft was the foundation of their very successful putting strokes, some going all the way back to the early 1900s. And these were putting strokes that had won twenty-four major championships between them—and had won Hagen, Casper, Smith, and Locke places in the World Golf Hall of Fame.

I found it especially revealing when the Metropolitan Section of the PGA of America recognized me with the Horton Smith Award for the first time, and I started to read about the man who had won the very first Masters, back when it was called the Augusta National Invitational. I also bought a book of his, *The Secret of Holing Putts*, and learned about "hooding" the putter. That's how he described "the necessary counterclockwise turn of the left wrist during the backswing." Smith said he applied that so he could keep the blade perpendicular or "square to the line" of the putt at all times.

I could see how "hooding" helped golfers keep their putter blades square. But I also noticed that as the lead wrist "hoods" the clubface, it also forces the shaft to lean forward. That creates negative loft, and that's what enables golfers to create topspin, or forward rotation.

Smith wrote about how other putting greats advocated "hooding," and suddenly, it became clear that all I had really done was *rediscover* a secret that pros like Smith knew about decades ago.

Once I realized that, I began devouring books on putting to see what else I could find. I read about Park, who won the British Open in 1887 and 1889 and was widely admired for his short game. He described the virtues of forward shaft lean and the way it helped impart the best possible rotation on a putted ball in a book published in 1920! I also discovered that the great Walter Hagen, who won eleven majors and was considered the best putter in the game during his playing heyday almost a century ago, often spoke of "hooding" the face of his putter to apply topspin to the ball. Smith found similar benefits to imparting forward rotation to his putts. The same is true for Casper and Locke, both of whom are still regarded as two of the best flatstick artists ever to play the game. Locke's favorite putter was an old, rusty-headed club with a hickory shaft, and he frequently talked of "hooking" his putts so that he could put topspin on the ball and produce that true, end-over-end forward rotation that is the key to good putting.

Forward rotation. Topspin. These were all keys to good putting, and these guys were creating those by using forward shaft lean to put negative loft on their putters. It seemed so simple, and it made so much sense. Good roll was the key to making putts. And the key to getting good roll was having an impact point high enough on the ball to impart forward rotation. And the best way to find that impact point each time was with negative loft.

Problem was, modern golf instructors had long ago forgotten the truth about negative loft. And it had been years since anyone had actively promoted or taught the concept. To be sure, I found the occasional comment by someone like Dave Stockton, who has to be considered among the best putters of his era, alluding to the performance benefits of putting that way. "It is easier to putt well when you start with your hands ahead of the ball, which is where the forward press puts them," he once wrote. But Stockton was very much in the minority. And so was I, even as I became a bigger and bigger proponent of negative loft and the forward shaft press.

I had gotten that way because I found that negative loft worked for me, and for my students. I was also getting more and more recognized for my teaching, especially as it related to putting. But I still didn't have the proof that my theories were right, or that the theories Horton Smith, Bobby Locke, Walter Hagen, and Willie Park had advanced well before me were valid. I didn't have anything to wave in front of a skeptical public and make my case undeniable.

So I went after proof. I commissioned a firm in Dallas to conduct a series of tests. I had been extolling the virtues of negative loft for seventeen years, knowing in my heart that I was right but not knowing for sure. It was time for me to get absolute confirmation of my ideas.

For those tests, Pete Piotrowski of P2 Golf in Dallas employed his putting device called "The Green Machine," which grips a putter and then produces a consistent stroke, much like the "Iron Byron" machine that the United States Golf Association uses to test golf clubs and balls. The device was calibrated to ensure that it struck a golf ball with sufficient force to produce a putt of 26 feet using a club with the 3 degrees of positive loft that is standard issue for most commercial putters. Why 26 feet? Because research told me that that was the average length of the first putt faced by most recreational golfers. I had the testers use seven different putters, and each putter was exactly the same in terms of head shape, weight, and length. There was only one difference, and that was loft. I started with a putter that featured 9 degrees of positive loft and went down in 2-degree increments, finishing with a putter that had -3 degrees.

LOFT	DISTANCE
9 DEGREES	15.5 FEET
7 DEGREES	19 FEET
5 DEGREES	23 FEET
3 DEGREES	26 FEET
1 DEGREE	31 FEET
-1 DEGREE	32 FEET
-3 DEGREES	33 FEET

(Margin of error: plus or minus 3 inches)

LOFT	DISTANCE DIFFERENTIALS
9 DEGREES TO 5 DEGREES	7.5 FEET
7 DEGREES TO 3 DEGREES	7 FEET
5 DEGREES TO 1 DEGREE	8 FEET
3 DEGREES TO -1 DEGREE	6 FEET
1 DEGREE TO -3 DEGREES	2 FEET

You may wonder why I insisted on using variances of 4 degrees (2 degrees on either side), and the answer is simple. Very few people—other than touring pros who participate in intense and regular practice sessions—are going to hit their putts with precisely the same loft each time. There are going to be some variances in their grips, stances, and strokes on a day-in and day-out basis. There are going to be fluctuations that can cause variances of a couple of degrees in your putter loft from a round you play Saturday afternoon to one you complete the following morning. And you're not even aware of them.

These things happen as a result of what I call my "rearview mirror" principle. Here's what I mean. I drive the same car every day, and at my age, I am neither shrinking nor growing. Nor has anyone else driven my car. Yet I often have to readjust my rearview mirror before I pull out of my driveway or leave the club. I may be a little looser one day, a little stiffer another, and consequently, I may sit differently in the seat of my car.

We're going to be that way when we play golf, too—feeling a little different physically from day to day, and being able to do some things a little better or differently based on that. Therefore, we're not always going to swing our woods and irons the exact same way, and we're not going to hold our putter and stroke our putts with absolute precision each day either. Weight distribution may change or ball position may vary from day to day, or even week to week. We need to be good where we are bad. So I built in that margin of 2 degrees on either side of each test to make the results as accurate—and reflective of those physical variables—as possible.

And what did those results show me? That the greater the positive loft in a putter, the shorter the distance the putt hit with the same stroke traveled. While a putt hit with 3 degrees of positive loft went 26 feet, for example, one stroked with 9 degrees of positive loft went only 15.5 feet. Conversely, a putt hit with the 3 degrees of negative loft I recommend consistently ran 33 feet. The ball rolled better because it had been struck at a higher impact point than the ones with positive loft. And it went significantly farther because it had forward rotation.

The testing also demonstrated that the distance variances are far greater from putt to putt as the percentage of loft is increased. Balls hit with the exact same stroke traveled 7 feet shorter when we went from positive 3 to positive 7 degrees of loft, for example, and 8 feet shorter when we moved from positive 1 degree to positive 5 degrees. But those discrepancies in distance lessened considerably as we applied less and less loft, as indicated by the results that showed putts rolling only 2 feet shorter when we moved from positive 1 degree of loft to negative 3 degrees.

The testing also showed me that a golf ball will break less when struck by a putter with -3 degrees of loft than one with 3 to 5 degrees of loft—on average, 2 to 3 inches less on a 10-foot putt. In addition, it demonstrated that mishits are not nearly as bad when made with that same amount of negative loft. In fact, a putt struck with 3 degrees of loft half an inch off-center lost about 10 percent of its distance, while one hit with 3 degrees of negative loft lost only 1 percent. In other words, a mishit on a putt that would normally go 26 feet with more than 3 degrees or more of loft causes you to lose two and a half feet of distance, while one with negative 3 degrees of loft will result in a loss of roughly 3 inches. That is next to nothing!

So, have I convinced you yet? Do you understand why I'm telling you to get negative with your putting loft? (And this is the only time I will ever tell you to get negative!)

What all those test findings proved, of course, is that the more forward spin you are able to impart to the ball, the better it will roll and the more consistent its speed and distance will be. They also demonstrated the ways in which forward rotation can help you achieve a more consistent stroke. That's because to roll the ball the same distance you have to make a bigger stroke with a putter having 3 or 4 degrees of positive loft than one with negative 3 degrees. And the bigger the stroke you have to make, the more errors you can introduce into the stroke itself and the less consistent your stroke will be. As any golfer facing a testy approach shot with a wedge or short iron knows, it's easier to make good contact with the ball using a shortened stroke. It's the same with putting—it's easier to hit the ball with the center of the clubface and at the correct impact point when you're taking a less exaggerated stroke.

Why do the testing? Why pour all that money and time into it? Because I was out there saying the world was round while everyone else was saying it was flat. Though I was considered one of the better teachers in the country, I couldn't get anyone other than my students to buy wholeheartedly into my ideas. I had videotapes demonstrating the validity of my findings as they related to negative loft and forward lean, and I wasn't shy about showing them to some very well-respected golf instructors. But I still couldn't get my peers to buy into my ideas. One guy even suggested my camera was broken.

Conventional wisdom said my theories were wrong, too. And by extension, Locke, Smith, Hagen, and Park as well. Or at the very least, it indicated that their teachings had been lost, sunk to the bottom of the ocean like a forgotten ship.

But the testing proved that I was right. That *they* were right. The secret was in the loft. The solution was, too. Negative loft, and my research confirmed that negative 3 degrees was best. Its simplicity did not diminish its significance. I felt that I had discovered the cure to the most debilitating, unnerving, depressing, and score-shredding disease in golf: the malignancy known as bad putting. I had found the answers to my questions.

CHAPTER FOUR

SPEED, ROLL, AND FORWARD AXIS OF ROTATION

NOTHING IS SO VITAL TO SUCCESSFUL PUTTING AS THE CLOSELY related matters of speed, roll, and axis of rotation. Good ball rotation gives you good roll. Good roll gives you good speed. And good speed gives you the best chance to make your putts. Speed, roll, and forward axis of rotation are golf's Big Three, and there is no way to putt with any sort of competency if you can't get them right.

Putting is all about speed, and when speed is not consistent, it is impossible to hole anything but a straight-on putt. And how many straight-on putts do you actually get in a round? Not many—research tells us that 92 percent of all first putts have some degree of break. Which means that only 8 percent of your first putts on a green are straight. That means that we have to play for break on a large majority of our putts, which means that we have to "give away" the hole—in other words, we have to hit the ball outside the hole.

What makes that prospect so daunting is that our putts are never more reliant on consistent speed to be successful than when we have to give away the hole. That's why speed is so important.

Streaky putters have inconsistent speed, so now is the time to ask yourself: Am I one of those golfers who has a great putting round one day, only to follow it with five less than spectacular rounds? Am I the type of golfer who makes everything I look at one morning, and then three-jacks my way around the course the next few times I tee it up? Am I pleasantly surprised when my Scotty Cameron gets hot, and quickly resigned to another so-so day when I miss a couple of early—and easy—chances at birdie? And do I blame those moments on the manhood-robbing whims of the Golf Gods, all those lip-outs and near misses and burners that scorch the edge of the cup?

You're like most golfers if you answered in the affirmative to those queries. But you don't have to be like most golfers.

Instead, you can appreciate that the root of most putting problems—and the key to most putting success—is speed. Even the best golfers in the world understand that—golfers like Tiger Woods. Something he said after the Deutsche Bank Open in the fall of 2010 was quite revealing. You remember how he was struggling back then. His wife had just divorced him. His game was agonizingly up and down. His putting was downright mediocre. But in the last round of that late-season event, his flatstick started to work again. Not surprising for a man with his golf IQ, Tiger knew exactly why. "I figured something out today," he said after his round. "Once I got my speed dialed in . . . I think I one-putted the last seven holes."

Once I got my speed dialed in? See, Tiger knows.

But enough about Tiger. What about you? Let's say you're an "end-spot" putter. You pick a spot around the hole at which to hit the ball, and then you putt your ball based on going that distance. You have to hit it that exact distance if you have any hope of it breaking into the hole. You have to control your speed, and not cede that control to the ground. You can't be popping balls up into the air, or allowing back-spin to check them up on the green, or letting the dips and bumps of the turf determine where your golf ball is going. You have to make sure that you get the ball to the spot you've picked out, and you have to do it time and time again. In order for you to be successful, in order for you to make more putts and post good scores, you have to have your speed down on every hole.

WHAT, THEN, IS THE BEST WAY TO ACHIEVE CONSISTENT SPEED? CREATE A
good roll. And you do that first by moving your hands forward once
you've gripped the putter and slightly hooding the face. That way, you
can produce the 3 degrees of negative putter loft I recommend. Then,
as you stroke the ball, you make contact with the center of the clubface
at a point that is at or just above the equator of the ball. That allows
you to impart a forward axis of rotation, one that produces topspin and
rolls the ball properly to the cup.

It's interesting when you think about putting, because it requires
us to make a very different stroke from others we execute in golf. The
ball doesn't compress on the putterface. The sole provider of speed is
the putterhead itself, and the hit must be made with the center of the
head at the proper contact point. The tempo must be consistent, too, as
well as the length of the putting stroke, which I like to consist of a
backswing to follow-through ratio of one to one and a half—in other
words, for every inch you move the club in the backswing, you should

follow through one and a half inches. The stroke must have more energy coming through the ball than going back. That way, you avoid deceleration. So if you take the putter back a foot, you should follow-through a foot and a half.

Horton Smith wrote about that perfect roll in *The Secret of Holing Putts*, which came out in 1961 and speaks to the ways that the great Bobby Locke influenced his thinking on that topic (and, by extension, Walter Hagen, who influenced Locke). Smith described the benefits of producing "correct, end-over-end roll" that would send the ball "on its way with topspin." He felt a putt rolling that way would hold its intended line better, adding that it "actually seems to hunt the cup."

That's a nice visual, isn't it? A ball that "hunts" the cup. I like that description, and I like the way Horton Smith makes his point about good, end-over-end rolls. The man knew what he was talking about, too. A former president of the PGA of America and a two-time winner of the Masters as well as twenty-eight PGA Tour titles, he would go years without three-putting. In fact, Gary Player says that he played with Horton more than a hundred times and never saw him three-jack once.

It's impossible to overemphasize the importance of a good roll like the one Smith writes about. A putt with good roll is one that moves with forward spin and has only one axis of rotation. It hugs the ground from the moment of impact and is barely lifted into the air. It proceeds to the hole in as steady and smooth a way as possible.

When I talk about axis of rotation, I mean the axis around which the ball rotates. A properly hit putt will have just one axis, in which the rotation is parallel to the ground and moving toward the target. You achieve that ideal rotation when you strike the ball at or above its equator. But if you hit the ball below the equator, you create a rotation in which the ball is spinning toward you. That's what happens when you strike a ball with positive loft. The loft causes the ball to hop into the air and initially spin with backward, or reverse, rotation. Once a ball hit that way finally settles on the ground, it does begin rolling toward the target. And it does so with a second axis of rotation, which causes all sorts of problems.

Reverse rotation forces the ball, in effect, to fight the direction the golfer intends it to travel on toward the hole. It also hands over control of the putt from the golfer to the ground, which tends to cause the ball to break more, especially if it lands on a bump or in a dip on the green.

The ball will bounce, rather than roll, down the line, affecting pace and direction and making it all but impossible to produce the consistent speed necessary for consistent putting.

But when you hit a ball with negative loft, you impart a consistent roll with a forward axis of rotation that is influenced by your stroke, not the ground. Your ball will break less than one hit with positive loft. You won't have to give away the hole so often, and you'll make more putts.

One of the more astounding things that I've learned in my years as a teacher is how many smart golfers have no clue what the sound, feel, or look of a "good roll" is—and how simply it can be achieved. But it's really not that difficult or complicated, and it all goes back to that very simple sequence that I mentioned early in this chapter. Use forward shaft lean to create 3 degrees of negative loft in your putter. Then make contact with the center of your putter at a point in the middle or just slightly above the equator of your ball. That'll produce that desired forward rotation. That'll allow your ball, as Horton Smith suggests, to really hunt the hole.

You'll know you've pulled it off when you hear the almost imperceptible sound that a well-struck ball makes and notice the purposeful path it takes as it immediately begins to roll. The ball isn't wobbling. Nor is it veering slightly off to one side or suddenly losing speed. Instead, it rolls to the spot you've chosen.

I got my first sense of what good roll is all about at the 1981 U.S. Open at Merion, where I worked as a volunteer at the scoreboard by the 17th green. I wasn't a big golfer then, but I'll never forget watching Ben Crenshaw on the practice green that week. For some reason, his putts seemed to have an extra foot to them compared to all the ones hit by the other pros. Crenshaw rolled the ball better. And it wasn't until years later that I realized he was a big forward-press guy. He believed in negative loft when it came to putting. He was all about consistent speed, and there was fluidity to his stroke and a smoothness to how his putts rolled. I had never seen anything like it, and I was fascinated by his ability. It was different. He was different. How was he able to do that? What did he know that others did not? I wanted to understand.

I try to help my students recognize a good roll by prescribing a very simple drill: Draw a line around the circumference of a golf ball and position it on the practice green so that line is horizontal to the ground.

If you're putting backspin on the ball, you'll notice that the line rotates backward—away from your target—just after impact. But if you're leaning your hands forward and creating just the right amount of negative loft with your putter at impact, you will be applying forward rotation, or topspin, and sending the ball toward the hole on a pure, tight roll, with the line you've drawn rotating in the same direction.

I've already mentioned the testing I commissioned a few years ago to prove my theories about negative loft, consistent speed, good roll, and a proper axis of rotation. And as you may recall, the bottom-line findings were quite clear: The more forward spin you can put on the ball, the more consistent your speed and distance will be. They clearly demonstrated that the reverse rotation initiated when golfers employ lofted putters actually takes away their control of the ball. And once a golfer loses control of speed and direction, he is far less likely to produce an accurate and successful putt.

To be sure, a ball hit with negative loft may still jump up from its original resting place when struck in that manner, but thanks to the topspin, the effect of the jump won't be as great. The ball will roll with more consistent speed and have a forward axis of rotation, enabling the golfer to retain more control over how far and fast his putts run. And that consistency and control will help him make more putts.

So be aware of speed, roll, and axis of rotation. One begets the other, which begets the other, which begets the third. They're the new Big Three of golf, and they're the keys to holing putts.

CHAPTER FIVE

READING THE GREENS

NOW THAT I'VE TOLD YOU ABOUT PROPER GRIP AND ALIGNMENT and everything I know about consistent speed and negative loft, it's time to get into some reading. Green reading, that is. And good green reading is one of the keys to good putting.

I say *one* of the keys, because the best green reader in golf is not going to make many putts if he can't start the ball on line and get his speed right. And he simply cannot read greens properly unless he has proper control of his putting pace, because if he doesn't have consistent pace, he can't possibly have any intelligent idea of where to hit his putts.

Concentrate on creating that consistent speed. At the same time, use the information I'm about to share on green reading. It's an advanced skill that takes some time and practice to acquire, as well as no small amount of the experience that comes with playing different courses and putting on various types of greens. But once you develop that proficiency, and combine it with a consistent rate of speed and a talent for getting your putts on line, you are on your way to becoming very good with the flatstick. Which, by the way, is why you bought this book, isn't it? To get better at putting. To lower your scores.

But you won't be able to do any of that if you don't learn how to read greens.

The first thing to understand about green reading is the importance of analyzing the property on which you are playing. Consider, for example, the location of the clubhouse. Most clubhouses are set on the highest point of a property so that they can provide the best views and the best drainage. That makes sense, doesn't it? If you bought property on which you wanted to build a house, you'd likely want the same thing. You'd want the best possible view, and you'd want a site that drained well, with the water moving away from you.

Well, the same is true with golf and country clubs, and you need to think about that as soon as you set foot on the property to play. Look at the direction in which the land drains from those spots, and you can discern the direction in which the grass on the greens throughout the course is lying—and subsequently the way in which a golf ball will likely roll on it.

Another element is the presence of bunkers. For one thing, bunkers around greens tend to have pretty significant lips that can raise up parts of the putting surfaces, and balls that roll anywhere near those tend to break sharply away from them. So you'd be wise to take those lips into account when you are looking at putts that have to travel in their vicinity. Also, keep in mind that golfers usually spray sand on the putting surface when they hit their bunker shots. That sand sinks into the green as the grass grows over it, building up those areas over time and creating subtle undulations that will also affect the way a golf ball rolls and breaks.

MUCH THE SAME THING HAPPENS WITH THE ROOTS OF TREES THAT ARE growing near greens. They can cause the ground to rise and fall very discreetly—and, if you're not aware of them, cause your putts to go off-line. Pay attention, then, to greens that are sheltered or bordered by trees. And consider the ways in which the roots of those oaks and maples and pines can ever so delicately create testy undulations in a putting surface.

You've no doubt heard that water is also an important factor— water as in ponds or lakes, rivers or sounds, even seas or oceans. But do you really know why? Well, greens tend to slope down toward bodies of water. That's because water often gathers in the lower sections of a property, areas often referred to as swales. And when it rains, the rainwater naturally goes to where the other water is—the low point. Which is downhill! What that means, of course, is that a golf ball will do the same thing—it'll break toward a pond or river. This is often the case even if the water isn't on a particular hole or is even some distance away. The mere presence of a lake or a sound can still tell you about even the slightest slopes in the land.

The key to so much of this is awareness—awareness of all the elements that can affect the way your golf ball rolls on the green. Stop thinking for a moment about that sweater you almost bought in the pro shop before your round. Don't worry for another second about those errands you have to run afterward. That joke you want to tell can wait until you get to the next tee. Now is the time to concentrate on the putt you're about to hit.

I work on my awareness even before I set foot on a course by considering the name of the place. A course with "dale" or "hill" in its name—like "Sunningdale" or "Round Hill," for example—will likely be hillier than a club with a name that includes the word "field," like "Fairfield." So I can expect the undulations on the greens at Sunningdale to be greater, and the breaks of my putts more significant, than at Fairfield.

I also look at the dates of when clubs were founded and courses were built. Minimal amounts of earth were moved when the old ones were constructed back in the 1920s and '30s, for example, and the primary tools used were horses and plows. That means the architects were much more reliant on working with what the property gave them. The intricacies of the land are thus easier to read and understand. It's more a matter of "what you see is what you get." In more modern times, however, golf course designers often move a ton of earth with bulldozers, and this can really alter the character of the property. That makes its inherent nature a bit artificial, and its quirks and tendencies a bit harder to discern.

My goal is to be very aware when I actually get to the greens. Walking across them as I get ready to line up my putt, or as my playing partner or opponents are lining up theirs, can frequently tell me a lot. My feet can sense dips and rises that I might not have seen as I approached the green. I can feel a little uphill tilt when it gets a bit harder to walk in one direction, and some downward slope when the going gets easier.

You can feel the same things if you just stop and think about it for a bit. Really. We all have that ability to sense hills and dales and dips and rises with our feet, and it all goes back to one of the first things we learned to do as humans, which was to walk. Walking was a process for us all. It took a period of time to learn and master, and one of the things we needed to figure out in order to do that was balance. Balance was a very instinctive thing, but it was also something we had to master. And as we developed our balance, we developed an ability to adjust our weight as we walked up and down hills, leaning into them either way so it was easier to walk. When we were children, our bodies and our brains could feel those changes in the terrain on which we were walking, and they can still feel them today. So take advantage of that. Use your senses to sort out the slopes and contours of the greens you're about to putt. You will begin to feel them. And once you feel them, you'll start to see them as well.

I SEE A LOT WHEN I WALK ACROSS A GREEN. I MAKE SURE THAT I NOT ONLY look at my putt from behind my ball, but from the side as well. That gives me a better sense of the distance I have to hit the ball, and it also provides me with another perspective on how flat or sloped the putting surface may be. I strive to get a complete picture of what the green is presenting me as a putter, and its true character is often only revealed after I've studied it from several different angles. I want to take it all in. I want to get to know what it's all about.

I mentioned other golfers a little while ago, and it's critical that you also pay attention to them when they putt. Take note of the pace at which the greens are running when they hit their putts, even if you're putting in an entirely different area. Look at the ways those Titleists are breaking. You'll notice that they don't move as much on slow greens, but that they'll break more sharply on a putting surface that's quicker. This will help you determine where to hit yours.

You should be able to learn something from every single putt that is played during a round. Think about why a putt comes up short or runs long. Did your opponent mishit it? Did he misjudge his speed? Listen, too, to what he or she says after a putt. Everyone is Jim Nantz on the golf course, especially when it comes to their own game. They can't help but comment on every shot. "I stubbed it!" "I hit that way too hard!" "I yanked it!" But those words should be more than mere chatter to you. They're important information to consider when it comes time to hit your putt. They speak to the misjudgment of your fellow players, or to their mishits. They inadvertently tell you something. When you hear these words, you should understand that your playing partners are telling you how they were fooled by the contours of the green, or how they erred on their strokes. So listen!

And be extra vigilant when a fellow golfer is putting more or less along the same line that you will be. That's like getting the final exam the day before you actually have to take it. Golfers talk about "going to school" on another player because it's an opportunity to learn something from a putt that's very similar to their own. And that can certainly help you when it's your turn.

But be respectful when that opportunity presents itself. Don't stand directly behind an opponent when he or she is putting, because that is considered bad form and can be quite distracting. Plus, it's against the rules. Stand off to the side until the ball has been struck. Then move in for a closer look.

Before you commit to the information that those putts provide, consider the stroke and the speed of the putt. Understand how your playing partner hit it as you look at the breaks and access the line. Make sure you appreciate how they hit their putts so you can get a complete representation of what is truly happening on the green.

And don't forget to be just as attentive when you hit your own putts. They will give you a lot of information that you can put to use on upcoming holes. Courses have overall characteristics that are repeated from green to green. Consider that. Be alert to them. Learn from your mistakes and your successes.

Before we move on to Chapter Six, let me offer you two other bits of advice. First, make sure you don't hold up your foursome, or the group behind you, by analyzing your putting line and those of your playing partners as though the Masters was on the line. Be thorough and thoughtful, but be expedient and efficient, too. Start reading your putts before it's your turn, while others in your group are doing the same thing. Then be ready to go when it is time for you to play. Don't overanalyze each shot. Don't be Judge Smails in *Caddyshack*. Hit the ball. While everyone is still young.

And second, don't forget your speed. Your consistent speed. Remember, the finest green reading in the world will not help you make many putts if your speed is not right.

There is only one way to grip your putter, and that is in the palms of your hands, not your fingers. You lessen wrist movement when you do that and eliminate face rotation, both of which allow you to produce consistent speed and direction more easily.

It is important to align the golf ball with your upper spine when you set up. Some golfers like to use their feet to gauge their positioning at address. But we can't always be sure we are spacing our feet the same distance every time. The position of our spine, however, never changes.

Of the three primary types of putting strokes, I prefer the one in which you go straight back and then straight through the golf ball. In my view, you have the most consistent and powerful transference of energy, from back-swing to impact to follow-through, with that style.

Good green reading is critical to good putting. Combine it with consistent speed and proper alignment, and you are well on your way to becoming a good putter.

The Claw is one of the best ways to save golfers who are suffering from that wretched malady know as the "yips."

Forward axis of rotation is a key to successful putting, and the best way to impart that on your putts is to make sure you always forward-press and apply negative 3 degrees of loft at impact.

Some of us have problems making consistent contact with our putters, and the Wooden Dowel drill is a great way to improve impact position and control the putter face. (See page 125 for more on this drill.)

Is your rhythm a little inconsistent when you putt? Then do what I do when that happens: Put a quarter in the cavity in the back of your putter and make some putts, being sure to be steady enough with your stroke so the coin does not fall out of the cavity when you do that. (See page 117 for more on the Coin in the Cavity drill.)

The Golf Ball Between Grip and Forearm drill is good for golfers whose wrists get a little overactive in the putting stroke, and it is designed to teach you how to use your shoulders, back, and chest instead. (See page 115 for more on this drill.)

CHAPTER SIX

BE POSITIVE— WITH YOUR MENTAL APPROACH

CHI CHI RODRIGUEZ WAS A GREAT PLAYER WHO WAS GOOD enough to be inducted into the World Golf Hall of Fame. He was also one of the game's best cutups, quick with a quip and acutely aware that he was as much entertainer as athlete. The Puerto Rico native with eight PGA Tour wins and twenty-two titles on the Champions Tour happened to be one of golf's most astute poet-philosophers, in a Yogi Berra sort of way, offering ideas and asides that often seemed a little goofy at first but upon reflection made a lot of sense.

"I've heard people say putting is 50 percent technique and 50 percent mental," Chi Chi once remarked. "But I really believe it is 50 percent technique and 90 percent positive thinking. That adds up to 140 percent, which is why nobody is 100 percent sure how to putt."

Chi Chi makes a great point here, and one thing I am 100 percent sure about is that a strong mental approach based on strong positive thinking is as much a part of successful putting as a sound stroke and a pure roll. In some ways, it may be even more important, as Chi Chi points out, for all the technique in the world won't do you much good if you can't get your mind right.

Don't get me wrong (or misinterpret Chi Chi): You must have both a solid putting technique and a strong mental approach in order to excel as a putter. You cannot have one without the other. I simply want to emphasize how important the mental elements are, especially those related to positive thinking. And my goal here is to take the physical principles built into a sound putting stroke and show how they can reenergize the mental principles that underlie good putting.

When I first started developing the concept for this book, I thought long and hard about how to approach both the mental and technical parts of putting. And I deemed the mental aspect so important that my working subtitle for this book dealt specifically and entirely with that matter. It was: "No Ifs, Ands, or Bad Putts." And while we decided in the end not to use it, those words nonetheless reflect how strongly I feel about honing your mental skills.

They also make some salient points that are worth breaking down. So let's do that!

"No Ifs" is a way of getting golfers to think of *when* something good will happen on the putting green, as opposed to *if*. *If* implies that the desired goal may never occur. As in "If I ever start making putts, my handicap will improve." A word I want you to use instead is "when." "When" suggests the desired goal is going to happen. There is no doubt that the desired result will occur, and the only unknown is the length of time it will take. "I will become a better player *when* I improve my putting." So as you talk to yourself, use the word "when," not "if."

"NO ANDS" IS THERE TO REMIND PLAYERS TO STAY FOCUSED ON THE task at hand, and to not let their minds get ahead of themselves by worrying about what might come next. In other words, concentrate on the first putt and don't fret about the next. "And" is a continuing-thought word. Deal with the present. Don't concern yourself with all the possibilities that might transpire—deal simply with the situation at hand. Forget about the past, and let the future be the result of solid thought in the present.

As for "No Bad Putts," this is a call to be strong and positive with your mental approach and to believe that there are no such things as bad putts, only bad reads.

That last one is really worth remembering. As golfers, we must accept the possibility that we're going to miss putts. But we must acknowledge the possibility of making them, too. The key is to pick a spot or line on the green—or some combination of the two—and commit to it. The ball may not go into the hole because the read was not exactly right. You might even get a bad bounce that sends it off line. But you still hit a good putt.

I think one of the most important things we can do as golfers is to not blame ourselves. We all make bad strokes at times. But we don't have to admit that. Once we tell ourselves we've made a bad stroke we begin analyzing, and then trouble sets in because we are suddenly and completely dealing with negatives. Deal with positives instead. When good things come out of your mind, good things will come out of your body.

And let me ask you this: Wouldn't you always want to tell yourself good things? To be your own best friend on the golf course? It sounds simple, I know. But it's hard to do unless you remember and are aware. Be encouraging, and be positive!

Golf is very much a game of vagaries. We want to be as precise and prepared as possible when we play it. With our techniques. With our equipment. With our distances and reads. But we're human, which means that we're not always the same, day to day, and not always at our best. We also strive to eliminate risk and chance when we play, but we can't possibly have total control of our situation. Golf isn't a sport that allows us to do that absolutely. There are just too many outside factors involved. Weather, to name just one. Rain and wind can impact our games, and so can temperature. Then there are the courses themselves, with their pitched fairways and contoured greens, their blind shots and downhill lies, their pot bunkers set in the middle of fairways, and their gnarly rough running right up to the edges of the greens. There are just so many things that can mess with even the most deftly hit shots.

We must take those vagaries into account whenever we play, and we must consider them when we consider our successes. We have to go with the flow if we want to have any hope of succeeding, because in the game of golf, there truly are things over which we have no power.

Perhaps no one has come to exemplify the importance of taking that laissez-faire approach, and the success it can bring, more than Tom Watson. Watson won five British Open Championships in his Hall of Fame career. All of those were played on great links layouts in the British Isles—where the wind often blows, where the fairways and greens run firm and fast, and where seemingly innocent bumps and mounds can send perfectly hit shots off line. Links golf can be a maddening experience for the uninitiated, and Watson did not care for it at all. In fact, he well remembers the first drive he ever hit on a Scottish links. It flew straight down the middle of the fairway, and then hit a mound, careening into a pot bunker. He admits to struggling with links golf from that point onward, and it wasn't until after he won his third Open Championship—that's right, his third!—that he said he learned how to "go with the flow." If a ball kicked into a bunker or got knocked down by a fierce wind or veered off line when it rolled across a ridge that he hadn't seen on the green, Watson just shook it off. He took note of how well he had hit the ball, then took what the course gave him and moved on to the next shot.

Tom Watson learned those important lessons on links golf courses. But they are applicable to any tracks we play and any shots we hit. Pick your target and focus on hitting it. Then let the chips fall where they may. If you get hurt by a spike mark you couldn't repair or a break you didn't see, forget it. Remember the good, solid putt you hit, and play on. Just make sure to maintain the purpose of the game, which is to hit your targets—and to do so with confidence.

Tom taught us all a lesson about confidence, and the mental aspect of putting, when he made that great run in 2009 at the British Open. You remember the scene, this nearly sixty-year-old man playing in the final group on the final day, needing only a par on the 72nd hole of the championship to become the oldest winner of a major tournament in golf history—and to accomplish one of the great athletic feats of all time. He hit his approach shot pure, but it just ran through the green and came to rest on the collar. Tom decided to putt the ball rather than chip it, and in the press conference immediately afterward he said, "I decided I was going to make sure I wasn't going to leave it short."

Well, he didn't leave it short, did he? In fact, he gunned it by the hole, and then failed to make his comebacker. He finished with a bogey to tie with Stewart Cink, and the subsequent playoff did not go well for him at all. All of which reminds us of the power of positive thinking and confidence. Don't think about not leaving it short. Think about hitting your target. Think of hitting it with the proper speed. Tom did what he told himself to do, which was wrong. And if the great Tom Watson can fall victim to that sort of defensive, negative thinking, so can we. We must all guard against that.

Confidence is so important in putting. You can feel yours grow when you make a couple of four-footers early in a round, and you know a key to your success stems from feeling confident over every shot. But I want you to come to the golf course with confidence. Don't wait for it to show up. Bring it! At no time can you stand over a putt with doubt and distrust and have much of a chance of making anything. You must learn how to feed off the assurances you give yourself in your mind, the confidence you bring each time you step over a putt— and figure out how to work your way through any negative thoughts that creep in. It does no good to stroke a ball with the possibility of failure racing through your head. Rather than focusing on failure, you need to accept the possibility of success.

I use a saying to describe that: Don't mind if you do. Embrace the fact that you are capable of being a good putter, that you can make putts. And don't mind if you do.

Of course there are going to be times when, try as you might, you're going to feel like you've made a bad putt, that you have failed. What you must do then is bounce back. Like a relief pitcher who has blown a save one night and has to come in to pitch the following evening. Or a quarterback who has to take his offense onto the field after throwing an interception the previous series. Acknowledge the miss. Accept the results that did not meet your hopes and expectations. Realize that doubts and breakdowns happen to all golfers, pro and amateur alike. Then move on to the next shot, the next putt. Have confidence. Think positively.

To use a combat analogy, you need armor to fight the war. And part of that armor is getting your mind right.

I take that approach with my television show, *The Golf Fix,* and when I say, "Let's *do* this!" I mean, in essence, "We're going to do this." Failure is not an option. We are going to figure out how to do something, and we are going to get it done. This is what I want you to think when you're putting: that something good *is* going to happen—not that you just hope it will.

Of course, the mental art of putting is more than just being positive and strong and steady. It is also knowing the type of putter you are—line or spot or somewhere in between—and understanding the best way you process information in your head as you stand over a ball on a green and get ready to stroke it. And you need to sort out that aspect of your game as much as you need to be negative with your putter loft—and, of course, positive with your mental approach.

We'll get into identifying your putting type later in this chapter. For now, let's focus some more on the importance of being positive. And so much of that comes down to a very simple philosophy: As you *think*, so you *become*. If you think positive thoughts, you have a much better chance of producing positive results. It also helps that those thoughts are consistent, too. Consistency in the mental part of putting is as critical as it is in the technical part. I want you to impart consistent speed on the Titleists you putt, and I want you to have consistent and positive thoughts as you do that.

The power of positive thinking is discussed so often that it's almost clichéd. But just because it's clichéd doesn't mean it's not true. The fact is, positive thinking works—especially in sports, and especially in golf.

Let me emphasize one thing: What you tell yourself does not have to be true. You just have to believe it. There are no shortages of success stories about golfers being better putters by being positive, and one of my favorites involves a member at Augusta National. He was a low-handicap player who drove the ball well and hit his irons pure. But he was having a terrible time with his putting, even though he knew and understood all the right techniques. He was also pretty good at reading those Augusta greens. We went to the practice putting green, and after watching him for a while, I could tell his stroke was in good shape. So I tried a different approach. I told him to go home every night and tell his wife he was becoming a great putter. I did not care how he actually played that day. I just wanted him to convey that message to her regularly. I told him that if he did that every day for a month, I wouldn't charge him for the lesson.

A few weeks went by, and this fellow shoots 67. That's five under par, and he said he made everything. He was beaming, and that was because he had become a great putter. Not because he had done anything with his putting stroke, but because he had started to believe in himself.

By making him tell his wife that he was a good putter, I had forced him to actually believe it. And it spoke to the importance of believing in oneself, and of how limiting negative thoughts can be. A good putting stroke made with bad thoughts in your head will result in a bad putt. But a bad putting stroke with good thoughts stands a much greater chance of success.

This was a real eureka moment, because it showed me for the first time just how important the mental part of putting was, and how it was so much more than just having a good putting stroke. I was encouraging my member to get positive without really understanding at the time how critical being positive was. I had a sense of its significance, but not much more. That incident changed everything for me, however, and I couldn't help but think of Chi Chi when it happened. Putting is 50 percent technique and 90 percent positive thinking. He was exactly right.

I practice what I preach as far as getting positive is concerned. In fact, it is part of my putting routine (and we will get into routines a bit later, too). When I stand over a ball, I tell myself I am the greatest athlete in the world. Of course, it can be argued rather convincingly that LeBron James is a better one. Tiger Woods, too. But neither of them is going to hit the ball for me. So I tell myself something that will allow me to perform at my best. I believe that. I believe the best athlete in the world hits his putts consistently well each time and always hits his spots. And because I believe that about myself, I feel I have nothing to worry about.

By the way, I am a great putter. Just ask me, and I will tell you so! Ask Brad Faxon the same question, and while he may not be so bold as to make the same claim out loud, you can bet he feels that way about that aspect of his game. You can bet that if he gets invited to compete in a putting contest, he will be there, and he will likely come out on top. He is one of the best putters ever, and he knows it. Which is part of the reason why he's so good.

Again, what you tell yourself does not have to be true. You just have to believe it.

It really makes sense, doesn't it? If we have someone telling us we're good, even if that someone is ourselves, we are more likely to perform better. If we feel good about what we're doing, we're much more likely to do it well. We're much more likely to succeed.

Interestingly, one of the keys to being positive is making sure that you don't get negative. And I use another little saying to emphasize that: If you're thinking *don't*, then *don't*. In other words, don't hit the ball if you're thinking that you're going to fail, that you're going to miss the putt, that you're going to stroke the ball ten feet past the hole. That's no way to be successful on the green, or anywhere on the golf course, for that matter. In fact, that's no way to be successful in life. So listen to what is going on in your head. Hear yourself, and the second the word "don't" crops up, *don't*. Don't hit the putt. Step away. Step back. And get your mind right.

Here's a good example of what I mean. There's a member at Sunningdale to whom I give a lesson every year the afternoon before our club championship begins. We do a putting drill in which he has to make ten putts in a row from ten feet. If he misses just one, he has to start again. In our session in 2006, he made five putts in a row and then missed his sixth. He did that four consecutive times. I could tell he was getting frustrated. So when he got to his sixth putt in the next sequence, I boldly suggested that he just start over now, because there was no way he was going to make that putt. I told him he was going to miss it because he was already telling himself that. He knew it. I knew it. So I wanted to put his brain in a better place, because what you put in your mind has to be good for your game if you intend to succeed. And you're the only one who can control the negative or positive thoughts that come in.

"What the hell are you trying to do to me?" he asked.

I said, "I'm only saying out loud what is obviously going on in your mind over that sixth putt. You're worrying about missing it again." I was trying to get him to understand that bad thoughts aren't necessarily bad as long as you don't have them while you're hitting the putt. When it comes time to stroke the ball, think about hitting the target, not missing it.

We worked hard on overcoming his negative thoughts and then figured out how to get positive ones into his head. That weekend, he played his way into the finals of our club championship, which entailed a 36-hole match. He was 2 up with three holes to go, and he had a key six-footer to halve the 34th hole. He stood over the ball, about to hit it, and then suddenly stepped back. Watching him, I knew exactly what had just happened. He had let some bad thoughts go through his mind just as he was about to hit the ball, so he backed off. Once he did that, he went through his routine again, and then made the putt. He did the same thing on the 35th hole, and won the club championship. And he's now won three club championships in a row.

What's the lesson there? That the key to being successful from a mental standpoint is only putting the thoughts in your brain that you want in your brain. Figure out what you want to tell yourself, and then do it. Whatever it is. You don't have to say it out loud. You don't have to share it with anyone. You just need to be consistent in telling it to yourself.

I'm the same way with my own game. Going back to the way I tell myself I am the best athlete in the world before I putt, if I have anything else in my mind but that belief as I get ready to hit the ball, I stop. I don't make my stroke. I step back and then start over. If something other than that mantra is in my head, that means I'm distracted. And when I'm distracted, chances are I'm not going to hit the ball well. So I don't hit it.

Now, I don't want you to get too crazy about this. I don't want to paralyze your putting game as you fight with yourself over the thoughts that are going through your mind. I don't want you act like a golfing version of Jim Carrey in the movie. *Me, Myself & Irene,* arguing back and forth with yourself while your playing partners wonder what sort of insanity has suddenly possessed their friend. Coolly, calmly, and efficiently control your mind so that you keep the positive thoughts first and foremost and the negative ones at bay. And if things start to get negative, step back and start over. Don't submit to the *don'ts.* Get rid of them, and then stroke the ball.

Remember this: Winners make things happen, while losers let them occur. That is true when it comes to creating and maintaining positive thoughts on the greens, and also to staving off the negative ones.

My students ask me all the time about putting routines and how they fit into the mental aspects of golf, and I think they're very important.

I get up every morning at a certain time. I know how long it will take me to get showered and dressed, and to drive to the Sunningdale Country Club where I'm the head PGA professional. I know how my day will start, and how everything will work, and there is a certain reassurance in that. But that reassurance can be shattered if, say, I get stuck in traffic. Or get a flat tire. An entire day can get messed up because the routine I've established is broken.

It's the same way with the golf swing, and with putting. Routine allows you to create and maintain consistency and comfort, and the more you do the same thing over and over again, the more chances you have for success.

Look at the pros. Tiger Woods has a routine. It may vary from year to year, but he does establish one, and he sticks to it when he hits his drives and irons and when he steps onto the green. Ever notice how Larry Mize wipes his putter blade on his pant leg every time before he putts, to clean the blade? That's part of his routine.

I have a very specific routine, too. I get behind the ball, pick the spot at which I'm going to aim, and then walk up to the ball itself. Just as I get to the ball, holding my putter in my right hand, I pull at my pant leg with my left hand. I take my grip, in the palms, of course, and then take a practice stroke while looking at the putterhead. Then I take one looking at my spot. At that point, I set up ready to hit the ball, moving my left foot and then my right foot into position. I put the putter blade behind the ball, look at the spot again, center my feet, look again, and then make my stroke.

Now, everyone will develop a different routine. Exactly what you do is less important than doing something that provides consistency and reassurance.

We did a segment on *The Golf Fix* one time about Tiger Woods and his routine. What we found is that, with very few exceptions, it took him seventeen seconds to stroke his putt once he was done with his reads and had begun going through his actual putting routine. It varied ever so slightly on occasion, as he would understandably take a bit longer with a thirty-footer than he would with a three-footer. But it was a very consistent seventeen seconds, with the same amount of practice strokes and looks to the target. They were identical each time.

Then we looked at Jack Nicklaus, and we discovered he was very consistent with his timing, too. He took about thirteen seconds every single time, from when he addressed the ball to when he hit it.

There were variations with Jack as there were with Tiger, depending on the length of the putt he faced. But it was more or less the same amount of time. And it was hard to not be impressed by the consistency they both showed in that regard. Especially when you think of a comment that Greg Norman once made after a round at the Masters when a reporter asked him who the best pressure putters were in the history of golf. Without hesitating, Norman said it was Tiger and Jack from six feet in, and Tiger when you got to fifteen feet or beyond.

Funny, isn't it, that the two best pressure putters in the history of the game, according to a pretty good putter in his own right, were two fellows with two very consistent putting routines?

Students often ask me why routines are important, and I think a big part of that is focus. Asking any of us to focus and perform at a high level on a golf course for four hours or more when we have work worries, family concerns, and Lord knows what else going on in our heads is asking a lot. A lot of us simply don't have the mental capability to disengage from reality and concentrate for that amount of time, especially since we're looking for golf to be an escape from everything else going on in our lives.

The fact is, we have to allow the brain some time to relax during a round, to take in the beauty and serenity of the golf course and the camaraderie of the foursome. But we also have to ask it to snap back into focus when it's time to hit a shot. That's where routines come into play. Routines are a way of reminding us to focus, and they're a way of allowing you to play better golf because you also enjoy it more.

Nick Price is a great example of someone who has long used a good routine to his advantage. There's not a more personable player in the game, and he's great fun during a round; chatty and generous and as amicable as your best friend in a Friday afternoon foursome. But when it comes time to hit, Nick quickly and efficiently gets into a zone by getting into a routine, preparing himself to play the next shot with the utmost concentration. As soon as he's done, though, he's back to being Mr. Personality, in the most unaffected way.

Routines allow Nick Price to stay focused but also have fun during a round, and we need to take this into consideration. If the very best in the world are doing something, then chances are it's a good idea. And if it's a good idea, then let's understand why, and let's do it ourselves.

It may take a while to figure out a routine that feels good to you, that works, and that's easy to employ. It's not necessarily just going to show up one day. Be patient. Enjoy the process. And put the routine to good use once you figure it out.

Another question that comes up all the time is: Should I always go back to the beginning of my routine if I'm ever distracted and have to step back from the ball? And the answer is a resounding "Yes!" Your routine is one of the things that helps get your mind right and helps make your mental approach positive and strong.

Of course, the greatest putting routine in the world won't help if you don't know what type of putter you are. By that I mean how your brain sees the ball and the green when you're putting. It's something that comes very much from the mind, and there are three basic kinds of putters: end-spot putters, line putters, and a combination of the two, line-spot putters. Understanding what you are—and how your brain works with your eyes to see a putt—is essential to becoming good at it. It will give you deep and valuable knowledge of your own game, and when it comes to putting, knowledge is confidence. Knowledge is power.

End-spot putters are those who feel most comfortable putting to a target. They pick out a spot near the hole and aim their putts there. Their eyes go from the ball to the spot and back again. Tiger is an end-spot putter, and the next time you see him putting on TV, watch how his eyes bounce back and forth from the target to the ball.

As the name implies, a line putter sees more of a line to the hole. It is not so much an end point as it is a directional point. Ben Crenshaw is one of those. You can see his eyes go up and down the line, focusing on the entirety of the path.

When I think of line putters, I often think of Raymond Floyd winning the 1986 U.S. Open at Shinnecock Hills. That final Sunday, he shot 66 and seemed to make every putt he stroked. He commented afterward that he was seeing the line so well he could smell the oil from the train. In other words, the putting line was like a set of train tracks to him, and he could clearly see, and smell, where it was on each green. That's more or less how line putters see things, too.

Then there's the person who is something of a hybrid—a line-spot putter—and what he feels most comfortable doing is picking out a spot where the break begins to occur on the line. In other words, he goes to a directional point.

One of the biggest flaws I see with people's putting is that they have no idea what type of putter they are, which means they have no idea how best to see where and how to hit their putts. That lack of knowledge and understanding can cause all sorts of doubts and uncertainty. And as I've said before, doubt and uncertainty do nothing good for your putting. What you need to do, then, is to go to the practice green and putt for a while to see what works and feels most right for you. Be cognizant that you are one of three types of putters. Take the time to figure out which one, by end-spot putting, by line-putting, and by picking out spots along the line. Sort out the one approach that is most successful for you, the one your mind tells you works best. And then become proficient at it.

Remember, this is a process and you will not solve anything in an afternoon. So enjoy the journey, too. It's a fact-finding mission, and while it may take some time, it will be time very well spent.

Another thing you need to sort out is whether you are a hard-line or soft-line putter. Hard-liners tend to play their putts with less break and greater speed. And when their putts don't go in, they stop two or three feet past the hole. Tiger Woods and Tom Watson used to be that way. On the other hand, soft-liners are maximum-break, minimum-speed players. Like Ben Crenshaw. When they miss, they miss by only a couple of inches. One approach is not necessarily better than the other. Rather, it's a case of preference and of sorting out what looks and feels best to you with a lot of practice.

Personally, I prefer playing maximum break. Which means I'm a soft-line putter. Part of that is because I like Crenshaw so much and have tried to model my putting stroke after his. When I putt, I tend to use a speed that will take my ball four to eight inches past the hole if it misses. So when I pick my spots—and I'm an end-spot putter, too—I pick ones that are that far past the hole.

I figured out that that approach worked for me years ago, and now my brain is so programmed to hit my putts at that speed that when I look at a putt and see a break of, say, four inches, that analysis is based on my usual speed of hitting a putt four to eight inches past.

I have a certainty of what my putting speed will be, and you need to be that way, too. When you stand over the ball, you need to be 100 percent certain of your speed and your target.

It comes down to a simple thing. You have to play the game of golf with intent, and you have to putt with intent. Forget about trying something; do it instead. One of my favorite movie lines is from *Star Wars: The Empire Strikes Back* when Yoda says: "Try not. Do or do not. There is no try." Here, with your putting, with your speed and targets, you must *do*. Don't *try!* "Try" is another word that you must purge from your vocabulary. Tell yourself what you want to do, not what you're going to *try* to do.

Not *doing* is one reason people struggle with their putting. Another is that they don't allow their eyes to properly assist their minds. So much of what we do in putting is focused on the hole and not hitting our line or spot. And golf is a game that is all about hitting targets. You do that with your drives and approach shots, and you need to do it with your putts. Pick your target, and hit it. The ball may not go into the hole, but it still may be a great putt. Great putts don't always go in. You just may have picked the wrong target, or hit a pitch mark, or rolled your ball over an indentation in the green that you didn't see.

Why is that important for our minds? Because we grade ourselves by the number of putts we have in a round. But the truth is, we've all had rounds where we've hit our targets and the ball just doesn't go in. And you can't fairly or accurately describe yourself as a bad putter if you're hitting the targets and your putts are just not dropping.

There is also much less drama when you tell yourself that you've missed a target, instead of saying that you missed a putt or hit a bad one. It somehow seems less of an issue in that context, and keeping it that way can help you stay positive when it's time to hit the next one.

And remember, what you tell yourself doesn't have to be true. You just have to believe it.

In the end, it all gets back to being positive, doesn't it? Be positive with your mental approach.

Before you move on to Chapter Seven, I want to leave you with one last thought. It's one that I've already covered, but it's one you need to remember as you move on. It's impossible to overestimate how important the mental aspect of putting is, and if you think that all you have to do to be successful with that part of the game is to get your stroke mechanics and technique down, you're very much mistaken. Read this chapter a few more times. Study it. Remember what Chi Chi said. Putting is 50 percent technique and 90 percent positive thinking.

He knew. And now you do, too.

CHAPTER SEVEN

GOOD-BYE, MR. YIPS

YOU'VE NO DOUBT SEEN IT HAPPEN. RIGHT IN THE MIDDLE OF your round, and right before your eyes. A friend carefully lines up his putt and then takes his stance. He brings his putter back a foot or two, but as he begins to move through the ball, his normally smooth stroke gets all twitchy and jerky, as if gremlins have suddenly taken control of his arms and hands.

You cringe, and your friend barely makes contact with the ball as he pushes it off to the right. It makes an odd, almost clunky sound and then stutters to a stop well short of the hole. You quickly turn your head, as though you've just witnessed a car wreck and don't want to look anymore. When you're finally able to gaze back at your friend, you shudder at his pained, panicked expression. He appears shaken. All color has drained from his face, and you understand why.

Your fellow golfer has the yips. And that means his golf world is falling apart.

Sadly, a lot of golfers catch this dreaded disease, in which a good putter goes bad and can no longer put a good stroke on the ball. But there's no reason to give up hope, or even the game for that matter, although those are very understandable reactions. As bad as the yips are, they are by no means incurable. In fact, the golf world is populated with players who have recovered from this insidious ailment. Many have done it several times, and those in recovery include not only your garden variety 36-handicappers but also some of the greatest golfers in the world.

Like Bernhard Langer. The Hall of Fame star from Germany has eighty-three professional wins worldwide, including two Masters (in 1985 and 1993) and both the Senior Open Championship (formerly the Senior British Open) and the U.S. Senior Open in 2010. But from that record and his remarkably consistent play over four decades, you wouldn't know that he has struggled with the yips on more than a few occasions. He won the '85 Masters using a conventional putting grip, for example. But by the time Langer had slipped on his second green jacket eight years later, the yips had compelled him to change to a lead-hand low, or cross-handed, putting grip in an effort to steady his stroke and once again putt at the professional level. That worked for a while, but then the yips came back with a vengeance, and Langer took to using a long putter to combat their debilitating effects. It was as though you could take his psychological golf temperature simply by considering the putting grip and stroke he was using at any given time. A new one usually meant that he'd had a new bout of the yips.

To be sure, putting has been quite a struggle for Langer over the years. He's had the yips. He's lost them. Then he's had them again. He's come down with the yips several times, but has always gotten over them. Which means that you can, too.

To beat the yips, you first need to understand that they arise from both physical and mental issues. The physical is really a matter of maintaining the optimum putter loft of negative 3 degrees when you hit the ball. Do that, and you'll be fine. But if you start altering your loft from putt to putt, you lose your sense of how far you hit the ball with the same energy each time. You lose your tempo as well as all feel for distance. Which means that you lose your ability to putt with any sort of success.

A golfer can often get "yippy" when he gets inconsistent with his putter loft, when he feels as though he's making the same stroke with the same energy with each putt but is actually getting very different results in terms of speed and distance because of slight and subtle changes that he's made to his hand positions. These changes not only alter the loft on the golfer's putterface; they also change where he makes contact with the ball and how far and fast the ball travels. That kind of inconsistency can sap a golfer's sense of how hard he has to stroke his putts and, far too often, he'll react to that uncertainty by decelerating as soon as he begins the stroke. That uncertainty can get so intense that he begins to flinch, twitch, and stutter. He has started to "yip."

It all comes down to speed and distance, and to appreciate how significant a role putter loft has in those matters, you need to recall what I learned from the testing I mentioned previously in this book. For starters, I found out that the greater the positive loft in a putter, the shorter the distance the putt hit with the same stroke traveled but that a golf ball hit with negative loft travels farther because negative loft gives it that highly coveted forward roll. The testing also demonstrated that the distance variances are far greater from putt to putt as the percentage of loft is increased. A ball hit with the exact same stroke traveled 7 feet shorter when we went from positive 3 to positive 7 degrees of loft, for example, and 8 shorter when we moved from positive 1 to positive 5. But those discrepancies in distance lessened considerably as we applied less and less loft, as indicated by results that showed putts rolling only 2 feet shorter when we moved from positive 1 degree of loft to negative 3 degrees.

What that proved to me is that you can be much more consistent with your distances when you use forward lean and apply negative loft to your putter. Even if you're off a degree or two, which golfers often are, the variances in distance are minimal. Again, 2 feet from negative 3 to positive 1. But the more positive loft you allow, the greater those distance variances become when you are understandably imprecise. It's 7 feet when you go from positive 3 degrees to positive 7.

The main thing to take away from these findings is how important consistent speed is to consistent putting—and to staving off the yips. And why does inconsistent speed lead to the yips? If you're making the same length stroke for, say, a 25-foot putt and it goes that distance one time, 30 feet the next, and 20 feet the time after that, how can you possibly know how to hit the putt correctly? You can't—and that doubt causes you to develop a trust issue between your body and your brain. You start yipping and jabbing and doing all sorts of things with your stroke because you just don't know how far your golf ball is going to travel each time. You start wondering about how short your putts will end up, or how far they'll run past the hole. Should you slow down or speed up? The only thing you do know is that the intended stroke is wrong, and you feel you need more or less energy at the last possible moment. You start asking yourself how hard to hit an uphill putt, and how soft to tap a downhiller, without ever really knowing the answer. All those questions start to spark in your head like an overloaded circuit board. It's "Danger, Will Robinson," because you just don't know what to do. So you end up yipping.

I'll say it again: The key is to create and maintain consistent speed to impart the same 3 degrees of negative loft on each putt you hit. The more you're able to do that, the more you'll be able to hit your putts with that loft consistently; and the more you're able to produce consistent speed, the less likely you are to ever have doubts about your putting stroke—or to have issues with the yips.

As Bernhard Langer has demonstrated, however, it's quite possible to recover from the yips and once again enjoy a happy golf life. He did that mostly by altering his grip, and that can be a very good solution for you. Perhaps the most popular approach is to switch to the so-called claw grip. For a right-handed player to adopt the claw, he needs to hold the putter in his left hand and use his open right hand, with the palm down, to steady the club as he strokes through the ball. Chris DiMarco turned to the claw after he lost his PGA Tour card in the mid-1990s, and not only did he work his way back onto the circuit soon after, but also got good enough to be ranked for a spell among the top ten in putting. He also came mighty close to winning a few majors, finishing second in the Masters, British Open, and PGA Championship within a three-year span.

The claw also helped 1989 British Open champion and thirteen-time PGA Tour winner Mark Calcavecchia regain his putting prowess when his flatstick began to falter. He started experimenting with it in early 2000, and the next winter the claw helped him win his first Tour event in three years.

I'm a big fan of the claw because it does such a good job of taking the fast-twitch muscles out of the equation. It creates a pushing action that stabilizes the putterface and promotes fluidity. It's also more comfortable to grip the putter with the claw by applying that all-essential forward lean, so it actually forces you to do that.

The claw is the first place I go with someone who is having issues with the yips. The hand position on the putter is so dramatically different that it actually takes a golfer right out of his comfort zone, the place he knows in golf so well, and brings him almost back to being a child, starting from scratch, with no history or preconceptions. It's nothing like the putting methods he's used before, so there are no old habits to fall into, no sudden reminders of the grip and stroke that were causing all of the yip problems. It's like starting over.

I ALSO LIKE THE WAY THE CLAW PROMOTES FLUIDITY. BY TAKING, IN effect, one hand off of the grip, you're able to swing it with better tempo because you're not gripping the club with both hands and you have less of a chance of jerking the putter. You're also stabilizing the face and giving yourself a better chance to be square at impact. The key is to make sure that all four fingers (but not your thumb) on the back hand are in a straight line parallel to the target line and perpendicular to the putterface.

I've been teaching for more than twenty-five years, and I've been majoring in putting instruction for the past fifteen. And I've never seen anyone yip a putt with the claw. It just doesn't happen.

The claw saves people. I mean it. Yips can ruin a golf game. They can put even the mentally strongest players into emotional tailspins. They can make what used to be a favorite recreation pure hell. They can drive you to drink. They can make you write bad checks.

I've put a number of my students into the claw over the years, and the results have been terrific. For example, one woman, who happened to be one of my better players, could not hit a putt into the cup from two feet. It was so bad that she started thinking seriously about quitting the game. Here was a person who loved to play so much, and who absolutely loved golf and loved to compete, but she could not hit a short putt without yipping terribly. It was heartbreaking to watch her go all to pieces like that, and things got so bad that no one at the club would give her a short putt anymore, no matter how short. Her anxiety was palpable. And so was her distress.

Eventually, she came to me for help. I got her to use the claw, and she almost immediately began making putts again. In fact, she started putting so well that she ended up winning three straight club championships. I thought that was great, but what was even better was helping someone who had loved golf so much find joy in it again—and find a way to keep playing.

A similar thing happened to one of my senior members. He was in his mid-sixties, more or less retired, and all he wanted to do in his later years was play golf. There he was, with the time and the money to tee it up to his heart's content, and he got the yips. He couldn't make a putt. It got to the point where everything had to be a "gimme" for him. He just could not put the ball into the hole anymore. He became very depressed by the whole situation and began to barely come to the club at all.

I saw him one day and talked him into coming out to the putting green with me. I asked him to hit ten putts from three feet with his putter, with his normal putting style. He missed all but one. Then I gave him a new putter, with a bit more weight to it, and showed him the claw. The first time around, he made eight of ten. Then we went to five feet, and pretty much the same thing happened. By the time we were done, he felt he could putt again. Which meant he could play golf again. So he started coming back to the club and getting back into his regular games with his friends. At first, he only used the claw from five feet in, and he was making everything. Then he took another lesson from me, and within a month, he was using the claw for every putt. He liked it that much. Now he even uses the claw when he chips.

CHANGING TO A CROSS-HANDED OR LEAD-HAND-LOW GRIP AS LANGER did after his first Masters win can work, too. But you still want to grip the club in the palm of your hands, and still need to apply forward lean and negative loft. The principle difference between that and the claw is that the trailing hand here provides most of the energy by pushing the club through the ball. With the lead-hand-low grip, it comes from a dragging motion, with the lead hand, which can stabilize a shaky stroke pretty well. You also tend to create a bit of forward shaft lean when you drag the club that way, which is good, too.

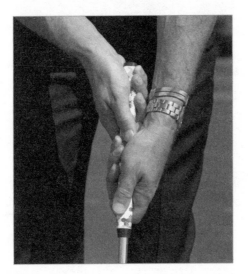

I find lead-hand low to be really effective for, say, right-handed people playing left-handed, or vice versa, because they're utilizing their strength, dragging the club through the ball with their strongest, or dominant, hand.

BELLY PUTTERS ARE EFFECTIVE AS WELL, LARGELY BECAUSE ANCHORING the butt of the putter in your belly keeps those fast twitch muscles from acting up. You're able to stabilize things that way. I do worry at times, however, that belly putters create a bit of positive loft when they stroke through the ball, and that loft will lead to inconsistencies in your roll. So be mindful of that.

As for even longer putters, they provide a pretty good antidote to the yips, too, as Langer discovered. But the key once again is to be sure to lean your hands forward enough so that you impart that 3 degrees of negative loft.

I believe it's important to look at the yips as more of a physical issue than a mental one. That's largely because people generally find it easier to address and then overcome something physical as opposed to something mental. The mind is just so complex, and our knowledge of it is quite limited. That makes it harder to figure it out than a very simple physical technique.

Still, the yips can and do become mental. Which is why we need to look closely at the reasons that cause them to happen and how to deal with them.

Many of our mental breakdowns in golf come from the pressures we put on ourselves to always have a successful outcome, and how we define what success is. For example, most people believe the only successful putts they make are those that go into the hole. But that sets them up for some pretty serious disappointment, because even good putts don't always go in. Sometimes you hit the ball with just the right amount of negative loft, just the right speed, and exactly to the target you've picked out. But the ball doesn't drop into the cup because it hits a spike mark and veers off, or doesn't break exactly the way you expected it to. We fall so in love with the idea that the ball has to go into the hole in order for the putt to be a success that we immediately blame ourselves for making a bad putt when that doesn't happen. We consider missing the putt to be a failure, and we can become so scared of failing that we lose all confidence in our ability to succeed. Doubt and distrust can creep in, and those sensations can easily evolve into the yips.

We need to think intelligently when we think of our putting. Every putt is not going to go into the hole. Every ball is not going to break exactly the way we want it to. We might even have some trouble getting our speed exactly right. It happens to us all. The key is to be reasonable about how we define success, to recognize that a putt can still be well struck even if it doesn't go into the hole, and to know that we physically have the ability to take care of the problems that arise. We don't have to let it get to us mentally. We don't have to fill our golf world with drama. If we get or feel a little yippy, if we start to worry about our distance, we don't have to panic. We only need to make very simple adjustments in loft and lean—and maybe in our grip. Then we'll be fine.

CHAPTER EIGHT

CUSTOMIZATION, AND THE BEST PUTTER FOR YOU

DON'T BE FOOLED BY THE MODERN PUTTER. IT MAY LOOK SIMPLE and uncomplicated. It may even appear to be the least sophisticated club in your bag. But it's actually a highly evolved piece of athletic equipment that combines cutting-edge technology with insightful design and eye-grabbing graphics.

It's truly something to behold.

It wasn't always that way, however. Centuries ago, shepherds banged the first putts when they turned over their staffs to smack rocks into rabbit holes. By the late 1800s, putters had become specialized clubs made specifically to play what had become the game of golf. And people back then generally carried two kinds—one with roughly 12 to 15 degrees of loft to launch long putts off the greens and another with only a few degrees of positive loft for those putts closer in. But those wooden clubs didn't look like much more than skinny hickory sticks with elongated knobs at the ends.

However, by the turn of the twentieth century, clubmakers had begun to make serious improvements in both the appearance and playability of putters. The breakthrough product was the Schenectady putter that Walter Travis used in 1904 to become the first American ever to win the British Amateur. The aluminum-headed, centered-shafted mallet worked so well that the R&A briefly banned its use. Later on came Calamity Jane—the offset, steel-blade putter that Bobby Jones wielded with such success in the 1920s and '30s. Wilson raised the technological bar even higher in the 1950s with its model 8802 putter, an austere blade with no heel-toe weighting and a favorite of both Arnold Palmer and, later, Ben Crenshaw. Phil Mickelson even uses a version of the 8802 today (albeit one made by a different manufacturer).

Next came Karsten Solheim and his fabled PING Anser, which featured heel-toe weighting and plumbing necks that set the technological tone in the putter category for years to come. Several decades after the Anser recorded its first Tour win (Julius Boros at the Phoenix Open in 1967), Scotty Cameron started taking putter design to even greater heights with his array of hand-milled masterpieces.

What this evolution led to was a veritable golden age for putters in the second half of the twentieth century, one that's continued to this day. Most modern putters are technical marvels that not only perform brilliantly but also look like works of art. We golfers have never had it so good.

Truth be told, golfers have it pretty good no matter what club they buy. Whether it's drivers, hybrids or fairway woods, wedges, or long irons, there is no shortage of choice when it comes to well-engineered golf gear that gives players every possible opportunity to perform well and to enjoy the game. What's unique about putters, however, is how long they lagged behind the development of other clubs—and this includes putter fitting and instruction. The flatstick was an afterthought for many, many years, but not anymore. Putters get plenty of attention today, because modern putters have so much to offer.

However, this isn't to say that every putter works for every golfer. In fact, there's a wide range of design and performance attributes in the putter market that is intended to appeal to a wide range of golfers. Bottom line, there are a number of factors that go into selecting the right putter. And golfers need to appreciate that. Off-the-rack shopping doesn't work. You're not picking up a pack of gum when you go into a golf shop looking for a new putter. You're not just buying a book or magazine. You're looking for a highly technical, incredibly refined golf club to perform what is easily the most critical part of the game.

Remember how we discussed the importance of putting in the beginning of this book? On average, putts account for 43 percent of all strokes in an 18-hole round. Great putting is what separates a great player from someone who is merely good enough to compete on the fringe of the PGA Tour. The best players on the top tours are not the longest hitters, although some of those certainly perform well. The best players are the best putters.

You need to think about that as you think about buying a putter. You need to put a lot of effort into the process. In fact, probably more than you might imagine, because it takes some work to find the putter that's right for you. A putter that fits your body, suits your stroke, and appeals to your eyes can make all the difference. And a bad one can be ruinous. It can actually be the root of all your putting problems.

Believe me, I know. And let me explain how by telling you a story. A story about the worst year of putting in my life.

It was 1996, and I had just started in my first head pro job, at the Birchwood Country Club in Westport, Connecticut. I considered myself a great putter at that point of my career, and one day I met a fellow who made putters. His work was highly regarded, and we got to talking. I told him I used a straight-back/straight-through stroke, and he felt I needed to use a face-balanced putter. I had always used a toe-hanged, heel-shafted putter, but this guy thought I should make the switch. So I did. And guess what? I started putting terribly. I couldn't putt it into the ocean from a boat. I stunk, and it was especially embarrassing because I had just begun my first job as a head PGA professional.

What did I do? I struggled for most of the golf season, and then switched back to my old putter. As soon as I did that, I started making everything again. What I came to realize was that the new putter simply didn't suit my stroke. The toe was lighter, it kept coming through impact faster, and I kept pulling balls to the left. But all that stopped as soon as I went back to my old putter.

I learned a big lesson in 1996. The kind of putter you use matters. The type of putter you buy makes a big difference. It can mean everything.

Let's start our study of putters by understanding the myriad design and performance possibilities that are available. Putters come in a slew of different head shapes and sizes, from minimalist blades and meaty mallets to futurist creations that look like they've come straight out of a NASA lab. They boast different lies and lofts, a host of weights and balances, and a variety of shaft positions and configurations. They even have graphics that give putters bold, bright, and sometimes edgy looks.

Do you want something with a center shaft, or one with a goose-neck offset? Do you prefer a putter that's 35 inches in length, or perhaps one a bit shorter? Do you fancy a flatstick with a thicker grip? And what about color? Does a steely shade of silver please your eyes at address more than a golden "honey-dipped" hue or something dark and Darth Vaderish? Weight is another matter. Do you prefer a heavy putter that may help give you a stronger sense of stability, or do you want one with a lighter feel that might enhance your touch on speedier putting surfaces?

The possibilities are truly endless, and it reminds me of how putting is such an individualistic part of golf, and how personalized players have long wanted their putters to be. The clubs must not only perform well but should be pleasing to look at and hold. And putter makers have gone to great lengths over the years to make sure we have a multitude of options—some of which are modest tweaks of time-honored designs, and others, radical reinventions of the category.

I am reminded of the depth and breadth of picks in that realm each time I go to Scotty Cameron's website to see what the master putter maker at Titleist has to offer. In 2010, for example, Scotty featured three primary lines—Studio Select, California, and Studio Select Kombi—as well as one Special Release, and they contained a total of nineteen putter models. That's right, nineteen! For that year alone! And there was an almost infinite number of custom combinations within that group, depending upon one's preferences for weight, graphics, length, and balance, to name just a few.

Looking at the putting universe as a whole, we see there are hundreds of choices. Not surprisingly, that broad selection is both good and bad. Good in that there is a putter for every golfer. Bad in that it creates "paradox of choice" confusion, where too many options tend to befuddle and mystify us. Especially when we're not exactly sure what we need or want.

So what's a golfer to do? The easy answer is: Get help! I'm happy to provide plenty of assistance here, laying out the basics of what you must consider as you search for the best possible putter for you. But I highly recommend that you also consult with a PGA professional, whether he works at your club, a nearby public-access course, or at a local off-course retailer. He has the knowledge and training to find the proper putter for your game and body type as well as for the course—or courses—that you typically play and the greens you putt. And by accompanying you on this journey, by being your putting Sherpa, he can discern what is best for you in ways that I can't because he's there with you. He's watching your stroke. He's listening to your feedback on feel, comfort, performance, and anything else you feel is relevant. He's there on the ground with you.

So, let me ask you a few questions: Have you ever been fit for a putter? And have you ever gone to a PGA professional to do that?

I assume the answer is probably "No!" for most of you, and that's no big deal as long as you do visit a PGA professional this time around. Why? Because the putter is the most complicated club in the bag to fit, and no one understands the complications as well as he or she does.

As a longtime PGA professional, I'd like to help you myself. But I can't be with you through the buying process. I can, however, give you all the information you need to be a highly educated consumer, and to understand the intricacies of putters and what you need to consider when you go to buy one. I can help you understand the challenges ahead of you. I can make you smarter.

My advice, then, is quite simple: Read this chapter a few times, and then go in for a putting fitting with a PGA professional.

PUTTER LENGTH

One of the first things you need to consider is putter length. Typically, putters run from 33 to 35 inches. The average putter used on the PGA Tour is just over 34 inches, because the average height for a professional on Tour is six feet, or just a shade over that, and a putter that length generally best fits a man that size. Interestingly, while the average recreational golfer is a bit shorter than a touring professional, most putters in everyday golf shops are 35 inches in length. So you need to think about how tall you are when you're checking out putters. If you pull a putter off the rack in a golf shop, it's probably too long.

Keep in mind, however, that this is a general rule and by no means absolute. You may be like Phil Mickelson, for example, who at 6'3" is taller than the average PGA Tour professional but uses a putter that's only 32 inches in length because he likes to putt with a bit more bend in his body than most. He obviously feels very comfortable putting that way and does very well with it. The key is having the knowledge of how height and putter length are related and figuring out what's best for you.

Putter length must also be examined when it comes to those conventional models that run from 33 to 35 inches and also belly and long putters. Most golfers I know use a conventional putter. But men and women with bad backs or who have issues with deceleration, or who are simply frustrated by a spate of poor putting and are looking for a change, often turn to the longer putters for relief.

HEAD SIZE AND STYLE

Head size and style are factors, too. Do you go with a blade? A mallet? Do you want a head that's perimeter-weighted and cavity-backed, or one that is toe-heel weighted? Part of the process is determining what looks good to you at address. But performance is a major factor as well. People who have issues with deceleration, for example, might find that a mallet-type putter with lots of backweight helps them get through the ball better. The size and heft of that style club is such that it almost swings itself. Many golfers also believe that mallet putters keep the face more stable through the hit. And most of them are designed with a higher MOI, or moment of inertia, for greater forgiveness on off-center hits. In other words, the sweet spot is bigger, and you need to hit the ball in the sweet spot in order to hit a good putt.

Additionally, putters that feature a large head can often help golfers with alignment issues because manufacturers are able to put longer sight lines on the top of the head.

In fact, sight lines are incredibly important when it comes to aim. And there are many kinds, from single lines to double lines to dots. What works most effectively for you is very personal, and it's one of those things that only a golfer can decide on after doing some serious product testing and seeing what feels and performs best for him.

PUTTER MAKERS PRODUCE A NUMBER OF NECK STYLES AND SHAFT positions as well. The three most popular neck styles are gooseneck, plumbing neck, and straight neck, and the primary shaft positions are heel-shafted, mid-shafted, and center-shafted. A few putters are even toe-shafted.

As the name implies, a straight neck goes directly into the putter-head, while both the gooseneck and plumbing neck have some bend and movement as well as offset. I like a gooseneck, for the way it suits both my eye and my straight-back/straight-through stroke.

As a rule, a gooseneck has less visual offset and provides the greatest amount of toe flow, which is the tendency of the putter head to flow from open to square to closed during the stroke. The amount of toe flow is dictated by where the axis of the shaft projects through the putterhead. If the head is heel-shafted—in other words, if the shaft projects through the heel of the head, as it does for most goosenecks—then the head has maximum toe flow. Conversely, a center-shafted putter has no toe flow and wants to remain square through the entire putting stroke.

As for a plumbing neck, it provides more visual offset and a more medium amount of toe flow. Most plumbing-neck putters are mid-shafted, which means they provide what I would call medium toe flow.

Toe flow is important when it comes to matching the head design to the player. So what might work best for you?

Theoretically, if your stroke has a natural arc, flowing from square at address to the inside, back to square at impact and back to inside on the follow-through, you have a natural toe flow and probably need a putter that does not have so much of that. If you tend to miss putts to the left (as a right-handed player), you probably need a putter with more toe weight and less toe flow, and you'd probably be better off with a plumbing neck. If your stroke is more straight back/straight-through, however, you probably need a putter with more face balance, one with a gooseneck or heel-shafting.

Obviously, performance is key as you work out which neck styles and shafting that are best for you. But aesthetics are important, too. We need to like what we're looking at when we address and stroke our putts. So don't be afraid to make decisions based in part on how the putter suits your eyes.

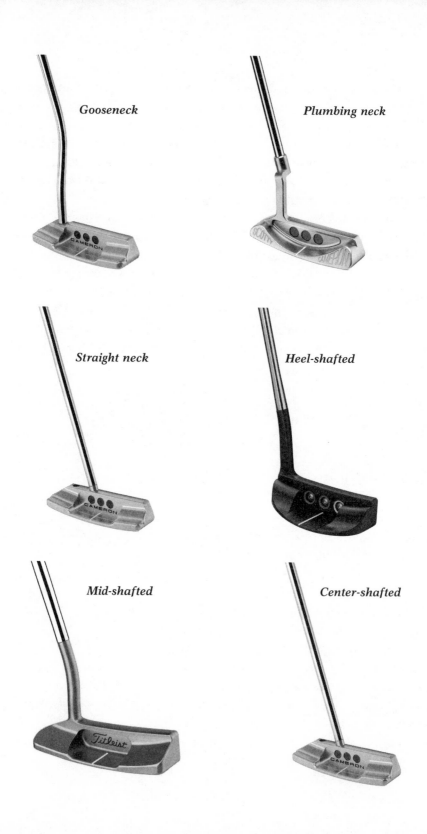

Gooseneck

Plumbing neck

Straight neck

Heel-shafted

Mid-shafted

Center-shafted

BALANCE OF THE PUTTERHEAD

Another consideration is the balance of the putterhead. There are so-called toe-hang putters, in which the toe hangs toward the floor when you balance the shaft in your hand or on your finger (because there is more weight in the toe) and the face points east or west. Others are face-balanced, and their faces have a north orientation. Common wisdom says that it's harder to keep the face of a toe-hang putter square throughout the stroke, which theoretically makes that style better suited for those who prefer an arcing stroke, with the toe fanning open and then closing but being square at impact. As for the face-balanced putter, the thinking is that it helps keep the face square to the target at all times, and that it's best for a golfer who favors the straight-back/straight-through stroke. Center-shafted putters will be face-balanced, while heel- and mid-shafted putters tend to be toe-hanged.

Believe it or not, the thickness of your putter grip is another critical matter. Some players like a standard-issue putter grip, but I prefer to build mine up a bit. It just feels more stable in my hands when I do that. Thicker grips on any kind of athletic equipment have a way of making the hands quieter. I need that because I have fast hands, mostly because I played a lot of sports growing up that required that, like baseball, squash, and tennis. If you're like me, you need to check that out.

Toe-hanged   *Face-balanced*

SWING WEIGHT

Now, let's cover the often overlooked and absolutely important subject of swing weight. Swing weight is the relationship between the weight of the putterhead and the weight of the handle where the grip is located. As a rule, the shorter the putter, the heavier the weight in the head needs to be. The slightest alteration can throw that off—and throw your putting off, too.

Say you find a 35-inch putter that you like. But it seems just a hair too long. So you get someone to cut it down an inch to make it fit better. Good idea, right? Wrong! Because as soon as it gets cut down, the swing weight changes. Suddenly, the putter is lighter, and suddenly you start having issues with tempo and stroke.

The same thing can happen if you fiddle with your grip. Consider this scenario: You hit some putts with a friend's club and decide that you like the way he's built up the grip. It's a little thicker than what you're used to and it feels good, so you think about doing the same to yours. But that could be disastrous, because random alterations like that can affect the balance of your putter and affect performance as a result.

PUTTER LOFT

Then, of course, there's the matter of loft. And if you don't know the loft you need by this point, you must have skipped a few chapters or been daydreaming throughout the book. Be aware that most putters have 3 or 4 degrees of positive loft. I like mine to have only 2 degrees, because I have 5 degrees of forward shaft lean, which gives me the optimum 3 degrees of negative loft.

AS WE BRING THIS CHAPTER TO A CLOSE, KEEP IN MIND WHAT A HIGHLY technical and personal instrument a putter is and how much time and thought must go into the purchase of one. I'm not trying to confuse you or overwhelm you with all this information. I just want to make sure you have all you need to make an informed decision, so you can ask the right questions when you walk into that golf shop and come away with the right putter.

Remember what happened to me when I bought the wrong putter. Remember the torturous time I had trying to make that flatstick work. It was my year of discontent, and it never would have happened had I picked up the putter that was right for me.

Now you know how to do what is right for you. The best thing you can do next is to see a PGA professional and get properly fitted.

CHAPTER NINE

USING THE VIDEO CAMERA

UNDERSTANDING HOW TO PROPERLY USE A VIDEO CAMERA IS ONE of the most important steps you can take toward becoming a great putter. In fact, I feel the camera is such an important tool for self-analysis in golf that I wrote a book about it, called *The Picture-Perfect Golf Swing,* in 2008. That volume describes the proper ways to use video when analyzing a full golf swing, and if you haven't read it, I strongly recommend you do. Not just because I wrote it (well, maybe a little bit because of that), but also because I believe in it so much. The book teaches the proper angles to take when you're using a camera, and also what to look for when reviewing your video. The best footage in the world will be useless unless you understand proper camera positioning and swing analysis.

Using a camera to analyze your putting stroke makes just as much sense. Given that most cell phones today have cameras, you probably have a camera on you all the time. So why not take it with you when you head to the putting green?

I can't begin to tell you how important this is, and its importance is the reason why I included it in this book. You have this book because you want to get better at putting, and it makes sense to think of using a camera to help you do that. The key is proper positioning and knowing what to look for once you've produced your footage.

VIDEOTAPING A PUTTING STROKE IS A LITTLE DIFFERENT FROM RE-cording a full swing. One reason is that the club isn't traveling as fast when you're putting. Another is that the golf ball isn't traveling as far. That means you can use a camera angle for putts that I do NOT recommend for the full swing: a shot taken from behind the hole. The two other angles are the same for putts and full swings: face-on and down-the-line. Taken together, these three angles will provide all the information you will need to properly perform—and analyze—the mechanics I described earlier in this book.

You might wonder at this point: How long should the putt I video-tape be? Good question! I suggest starting with a nine- or ten-footer. That's long enough to show all the good and bad that's occurring in your putting stroke. Let me emphasize, however, that you may find different successes and struggles with a variety of different-length putts, so videotape those lengths as well. Examine why you putt well from 25 feet, but struggle from 6 feet. Videotape both, and see what's different between the two. Don't just videotape the putts with which you have issues. Record the ones in which you have confidence, too—that will teach you a lot.

As an aside, you should know that I use my video camera exten-sively not only when I teach but also when I'm working on my own game. It's how I keep my stroke in good form, and it allows me to ensure that I never get too far away from the proper mechanics that provide for great putting. Tour professionals also use video for all aspects of their game—especially putting—as do the top clubmakers, who fit those pros for equipment in an effort to give them the best chances for success on Tour.

Video works, it is important, and it will help you become a better putter—I promise!

THERE ARE TWO PRIMARY HEIGHTS AT WHICH THE CAMERA SHOULD BE positioned when videotaping face-on. The first is waist-high, and the other is with the camera just off the ground. The purpose of the camera at waist height is to make sure that your pre-swing mechanics are correct. You must be consistent with things such as ball position, weight distribution, and shaft lean if you want to be successful. And to ensure that you're consistent, you need to check them often.

The waist-high angle also shows flaws that may occur during the stroke, such as adding loft to the putterface, flipping the wrist, decelerating, or losing that optimum 3 degrees of negative loft. These are all issues that need to be monitored, and any of them can kill your ability to putt consistently well. In addition, this angle will show what the head and body are doing. Excessive movement, for example, will cause serious inconsistency, and when you can see your flaws, you'll become more aware of what it feels like when you're moving improperly.

The other face-on angle, with the camera just off the ground, allows you to see the movement of the putterhead. It will show you the tempo of the stroke and the face angle at impact, and it'll give you feedback on the length of the stroke and the angle of the puttershaft at impact. As I said, one of the most harmful occurrences in a poor putting stroke is deceleration. With the camera at this angle and this close to the stroke, you can measure how far back and through the putterhead is traveling. You'll also get an up-close look at the negative effects that deceleration can have on the golf ball.

THIS FACE-ON, CLOSE-TO-THE-GROUND ANGLE ALSO ENABLES YOU TO see what the golf ball is doing when struck by the putterhead. The key, however, is to mark the ball correctly so that you can properly examine the way it moves. To do that, you need to draw horizontal and vertical lines on the ball. Make sure the lines intersect. This will create what looks like a plus sign. Next, you should position the ball in a way that shows the plus sign, as I've shown in the picture. You can now see what's happening to the golf ball at and after impact, and shooting from this angle with the golf ball marked this way provides all the information you need. You'll see how the lines are moving. Is the horizontal line turning toward the target, or is it spinning opposite to the direction in which the ball is traveling? Is the vertical line getting closer to the camera and spinning with sidespin?

THE FACE-ON ANGLE IS ONE I OFTEN USE WHEN I GIVE LESSONS. IT allows me to explain to my students the cause and effect of a poor putting stroke. I can see the angle between the putterface and the golf ball. I can also see how the ball reacts to the impact. The closeness of the camera shows the angle of the clubshaft, and as the angle of the shaft leans away from the hole, the impact point gets lower on both the ball and the clubface. This low impact point shows how the ball rotates away from the hole off the putterface. It also shows how the ball becomes airborne immediately following impact.

AS YOUR TECHNIQUE GETS BETTER, THE BALL STAYS CLOSER TO THE ground and begins rotating toward the hole after impact. This is the proper rotation that you want.

Now it's time to talk about the down-the-line angle and the two heights I use for that. First is waist-high. I start with this because it shows what the body looks like at address. Remember, pre-swing is the most important part of the analysis. You have to see how the body is positioned. Any issues you may be having could be the result of poor posture. Don't overlook the most obvious factor—setup.

So what are you looking for? The list is long. And every item is very important. Always focus your attention from the ground up. It will help create a habit in your self-diagnosis and provide for consistent thoroughness. It's what I do when I give a lesson—I make a ground-to-head analysis.

All of this is information that I've discussed throughout this book. Begin with the balance in your feet. The toe-to-heel relationship. What the lower body looks like. Is the grip in the palm of your hands instead of the fingers? When the grip is correct, the hands will be relaxed. You'll see the clubshaft-to-forearm relationship. Remember, what you want is to have the clubshaft and the trailing forearm in the same plane. Next, you're looking at whether the back is flat or rounded. What does the shoulder line look like? Are the eyes in the correct position? I could keep going, but I think you get the point. Make sure that you're precise with your setup position, and examine it every time you videotape your putting.

WHEN YOU LOOK AT YOUR IN-SWING FROM THE DOWN-THE-LINE ANGLE, you'll see the path of the forearms, the hands, and finally the clubhead in both the backswing and through-swing. The movement of the shoulders can be seen very easily, and the movement of the head will be clear. This view will provide most of the information you need, and it's an angle I use a large part of the time when giving a putting lesson.

THE ANGLE I LIKE TO USE WHEN LOOKING AT THE PATH OF THE PUTTER IS the low, down-the-line angle. I want the camera about six to eight inches off the ground and positioned precisely on the target line. You're looking to see what the putter path is, and as a result, you must have the camera directly on the path. If you're off on the angle, it will distort the appearance of the path of the putter. You may end up trying to fix a problem that doesn't exist.

THE FINAL ANGLE I RECOMMEND IS BEHIND THE HOLE AND DOWN THE line. That is another important angle when you're trying to see what the golf ball is doing after impact. Make sure to position the plus sign on your ball so that it's facing the camera. This will show whether the face has loft on it at impact, and whether it's square. If the face is properly de-lofted, the horizontal line will turn toward the ground. If there is loft on the face, the horizontal line will turn up, and the ball will jump up into the air. When the face is aiming to the left at impact, the vertical line will rotate to the left. If the face is aiming to the right at impact, the vertical line will rotate to the right.

The rotation of the ball is very easy to see and understand if you've positioned the plus sign properly. You must make sure that the horizontal line is indeed horizontal and the vertical line vertical. I know it sounds obvious, but it takes great care to get it right. It's easy to be lazy, and being lazy will not help you do that. Be diligent in your positioning of the golf ball. I can't emphasize it enough. But keep in mind that the position of the camera is equally important.

In many ways, those last words sum up this entire chapter. The best way to truly know what's going on in your putting stroke is to use video. Video gives you a way to properly analyze your stroke and determine the best ways to improve it. It also enables you to keep a record of those improvements over time. But you must use it wisely. Be precise when placing your camera and when choosing the angles from which you'd like to shoot. It'll help you become a much better and more consistent putter.

CHAPTER TEN

DRILLS, GAMES, AND PRACTICE

THE BEST WAY TO BECOME A BETTER PUTTER IS TO STUDY THE techniques I have outlined in this book—and then learn how to execute them correctly. And the best way to do that is through proper drills, games, and practice.

Two decades of teaching have shown me that most golfers have no idea how to practice putting. They also don't appreciate how much it can help their performance on the golf course and how much fun they'll have as a result, because proper practice will help them become better golfers.

It all stems from one basic premise: You get good at doing things by doing them a lot. Having the correct information to perform a task is critical. But if you are unable to apply that data, you will not improve. You only get good through practice and repetition. We all know that just going to class will not make you smarter. You must study! You must do your homework!

It's the same with athletics. Why do you think Major League Baseball teams have spring training? To determine the personnel makeup of their squads for the upcoming season, of course. But it's also designed to give players the chance to drill and practice, to work on performance techniques so that they become better pitchers, batters, fielders, and, eventually, all-around better baseball players. And that work doesn't end when spring training does. All season long, major leaguers are taking batting practice and infield practice. They're throwing in front of their pitching coaches in the bullpens. They're doing these things to reinforce the good techniques that they've learned over the years and the good habits they've developed. They do this so that they can get even better at something they already do very well.

Hang around professional golfers during a tournament, and you'll see the same level of dedication. They hit dozens of balls on the range before they head out to play. They putt and chip, too. Those same golfers also return to the range or putting green when their rounds are done, no matter how well or poorly they've scored. They know that consistent and efficient practice is key to being able to compete at the highest possible level. They know that practice is the only way that they can compete with the very best golfers in the world.

It is so much about practice for them. So shouldn't you be thinking about practicing, too?

The answer is yes! And I promise that by working hard on your putting technique—and by working on the drills and games that I detail at the end of this chapter—you will become the putter you want to be.

There are two primary reasons why golfers struggle with their putting. One, of course, is bad technique. But technique should no longer be an issue if you've been reading this book carefully. The other is that most people simply don't know how to practice putting. They don't know what to do when they go to a putting green. They hit a few balls without rhyme or reason, and then they head to the first tee. They're often just killing time. They're getting bored, they're losing focus, they're not changing or improving a thing.

Practice in and of itself is important. But it's only effective if you know what to practice and the best ways to do it. You never see a tour professional randomly hitting balls on a practice green. He or she is always working on something. They're performing a specific drill or playing a particular game. They're concentrating on developing good putting habits and reinforcing them so that those habits are easily transferred to the golf course during competition. They're correcting flaws. They're putting with purpose, with intent, and they know that the more they reinforce those good techniques, the better they'll perform. They understand how to practice, as well as what to practice, and that's something that all golfers need to consider. Doing so will help you become a better player. It will also make your practice time that much more fun.

It's critical that you understand all of these things, because you should practice your putting every time you go to the golf course. Touring professionals spend as much as three-quarters of their practice time working on their short games. They know and appreciate the importance of putting. But everyday amateurs spend 80 or 90 percent of their practice time smacking woods and irons on the range. They're rarely on the putting green, and when they are, they're usually hitting their golf balls without consideration or purpose. As I've mentioned previously, they're mostly just killing time.

There are some reasons why recreational golfers act that way. For one thing, they rarely take putting lessons, so they have no idea what to do to improve upon their putting or how to practice it. In fact, the average player takes only one putting lesson every four years. As a result, he never learns anything about that part of the game from the people who know the most about it—his PGA professionals—because he never asks for help. (Or he doesn't accept it when it's offered.)

Another problem is that people in golf rarely talk about practice—and when they do, they make it sound more like a chore than anything else. Listen to the commentators on TV. Read the golf magazines. Everybody's offering "tips." But very few people are talking about practicing—especially as it relates to putting. So it's not something that comes immediately to mind for most golfers. But it should, because as I've mentioned before, good putting is the key to good golf.

The first step to understanding the virtues of practicing your putting, and doing it the right way, is to appreciate that there are three different types of putting practice. One takes place before a round, another comes after you play, and the third is the practice you do when you go to the golf course strictly to work on your game.

As you would expect, pre-round practice sessions aren't generally very long, since they take place in the short period of time just before you head out to the course. Consequently, I suggest that you keep them simple and focused. One of the most important things you can do here is work on your speed and get a feel for the greens you're about to play. A good drill for that, which I detail later in this chapter, is what I call the "Pace Maker," in which you put a pair of tees in the ground and hit putts from various distances, trying to get each putt as close as possible to the imaginary line that runs between the tees.

Another sensible idea at this time is to work on tempo, and one way to do that is with the "Coin in the Cavity" drill. That's when you put a coin in the cavity behind the putterface and stroke your putts so that the coin doesn't slip from that spot. Once you can do that, you're putting with good tempo.

Pre-round putting is a good way to build confidence for the coming round, so I also recommend that you go through a simple drill of making, say, five putts in a row from five feet, then moving to another position once you've done that.

Golfers who have been working on a drill to correct a flaw in their putting may want to do a bit of that before a round, too, and I think that's a good idea because it reinforces the good habit that they've been trying to develop.

Post-round practice usually entails a couple of different things. One is a continuation of any drills or games that you've been employing to correct a flaw and/or develop a good habit. And the other is to address a problem that arose that day on the golf course. Perhaps you were pushing all of your putts to the right. Or maybe your speed was way off. Whatever the issue, that is a very good time to take care of it.

Post-round practice will certainly take longer than anything you do before a round, which is why I like the idea of mixing things up a bit during those sessions. Work on the drills that you've done before. Then go to the ones that will help you deal with the putting problems that surfaced that day. Then go back to the old drills. That way, you stay focused and keep the purpose and intent of the session strong.

I also like ending a post-round practice with a game in which I have to make, say, ten putts in a row from ten feet. Something fun and competitive before I stop, something I can really focus on and use to help put all of the things I've been working on that day to good use. Something that will also build up a lot of confidence for the next time I play.

Finally, there's what I consider to be strict practice. As a rule, this is longer than the pre- or post-round sessions, and the main idea is to work on the areas of your putting with which you've been struggling. So I suggest starting with the drills that address those issues. Just remember, the goal is purposeful practice. Don't rush. Allow time to develop those good habits. Let the drills work. What I like to do is to begin my practice session with drills that relate to the parts of my putting I need to address and to continue working on them until I see some improvement. Then I get into some games, ones that simulate on-course situations and help keep me very engaged. After that, I go back to my drills to reinforce what I was working on in the beginning. It's a way to get it all a bit more ingrained in my system, and also to see if I have indeed improved. I also think that this back and forth makes the one or two hours I'm spending in a practice session seem a little less monotonous and a little more fun. And I want practice to be fun, because the more you practice, the better you'll putt.

I've spoken through the course of the book of the importance of your putting speed. I want to emphasize again that without speed, you simply cannot be a consistently good putter. You may have moments when you putt well or even days when you feel like you're the best putter in the world. But good putting is not about moments. It's about consistency.

Now, for the drills and games. These are my favorites, and I've separated them into seven different categories:

1. Setup/Pre-swing
2. Puttershaft Lean
3. Tempo
4. Face
5. Path
6. Speed/Distance Control
7. Games

Any and all of these will help you become a great putter. But you'll no doubt find drills that speak specifically to *your* issues as a putter, and those are the ones you should perform first.

I. SETUP/PRE-SWING

Ball Drop from Eyes

PROBLEM: Not sure if you're the correct distance from the ball

PURPOSE: Ensure that your setup position is consistent

PROCEDURE: Remember, the most important part of being consistent with your putting is being consistent with your pre-swing. Take an extra golf ball into one of your hands. Set up to hit a putt while holding the extra ball. Before you hit the putt, hold the extra ball to the bridge of your nose, then release it and see where it strikes the ground. It should land on or near the ball you're about to putt. If it lands inside the target line, it shouldn't be more than one ball inside the heel of the putter. If it does, you're too far from the ball. The reasons for—and the effects of—being too far from the ball are numerous, and you should consult Chapter One, where I talk about proper setup.

Puttershaft Lean

PROBLEM: Inconsistent distance control

PURPOSE: Create the same puttershaft lean at address

PROCEDURE: You first must establish a consistent setup position, particularly in relation to the ball. As I mentioned earlier in the book, I like the ball at address to be directly in line with my upper spine. Once you've done that, creating proper shaft lean is simple. Make sure that at address, the bottom part of the grip, where the grip meets the shaft, is positioned ahead of the golf ball from your eye line. In other words, when you look down at the grip at address, the entire grip should be ahead of the golf ball. This way, you'll know that you've set up with the proper amount of shaft lean.

2. PUTTERSHAFT LEAN

Band-Aid Your Impact Point

PROBLEM: A consistently low impact point

PURPOSE: Raise the impact point, and consistently roll the ball properly

PROCEDURE: All you need here is a 1" x 3" Band-Aid. Apply it to the face of the putter so that it runs lengthwise from toe to heel. Make sure that the Band-Aid covers the bottom quarter-inch of the putterface. Now you're ready to hit putts. The goal is to hit the ball and miss the Band-Aid. The only way you'll be able to do this is to lean the puttershaft forward at address. Then you must maintain the shaft lean throughout the stroke. If you don't lean the shaft properly, you'll hit the Band-Aid. If you flip your wrists through the stroke, you'll also hit the Band-Aid. Basically, anytime the puttershaft is leaning backward you'll strike the Band-Aid. In order to get the ball rolling as soon as possible, and with the proper forward rotation, the impact point on the ball and on the face needs to be high. This is an excellent drill because it gives you immediate feedback on where your impact point is.

Running One-Hander

PROBLEM: Inability to maintain puttershaft lean through contact

PURPOSE: Be consistent with the roll of the ball off the putterface

PROCEDURE: Assume your normal setup position, with both hands properly on the putter. Now take your bottom hand, or trailing hand, off the club and make your stroke, feeling the pull of the lead hand. You'll also be able to feel how the shaft of the putter leans forward during the stroke and through contact. This is a drill that's good to do on a regular basis and great before a round of golf, both to practice forward shaft lean and to help with your tempo. When you make a stroke with the lead hand only, the tempo of the stroke will be consistent and smooth. If you watch Tiger Woods on the putting green before a round, you can see him perform this drill. If it's good enough for Tiger, it's good enough for you!

Once you've done this for about ten minutes with the lead hand, switch and putt only with the trailing hand. This is good for feeling the push of the trailing hand, as well as for making sure that the grip of the trailing hand is correct. You'll also feel the putter release properly, which gives the ball true roll.

Golf Ball Between Grip and Forearm

PROBLEM: Overactive wrists in the putting stroke

PURPOSE: Keep the wrists firm through the putting stroke

PROCEDURE: This is a very simple but important drill, and it's similar to the Drive with Tempo drill (page 120). It's designed to teach you how to use your shoulders, back, and chest rather than your wrists to make a putting stroke. Grip down on the putter so roughly four inches of grip extends above your lead hand. Place a ball between your wrist and the putter shaft. Make a putting stroke, and keep the golf ball in position throughout the stroke. After you've made a number of practice strokes, it's time to hit some actual putts. Make sure to keep the ball between your wrist and forearm throughout the stroke—if the ball moves or drops out, you're too active with your wrists. This is a drill that I always come back to. It's one of my favorites!

3. TEMPO

Coin in the Cavity

PROBLEM: Inconsistent rhythm in the putting stroke

PURPOSE: Create consistent distance control

PROCEDURE: Place a coin, preferably a quarter, in the cavity at the back of your putter. As you make practice putting strokes, keep the coin in the cavity. After you've had some practice with the stroke, introduce a golf ball. Once again, the goal of the drill is to keep the coin in the cavity throughout the stroke. If the coin falls out during the backswing, your transition from backswing to through-swing is too abrupt and will lead to inconsistent distance control. As your putting stroke gets smoother, your distance control will improve. And as your tempo improves, you'll find that the contact between the putterface and ball improves. This is great because your ability to hit the ball in the center of the putterface is critical for controlling distance.

Drive with Tempo

PROBLEM: Inconsistent rhythm in the putting stroke

PURPOSE: Keep the wrists firm throughout the putting stroke

PROCEDURE: Take your driver and turn it upside down. Yes, your driver! Place the grip in the cavity of the putterhead and lean the driver head against your lead arm. Make sure that the shaft of the putter and the shaft of the driver are parallel. Then make a putting stroke, keeping both shafts parallel throughout the entire stroke. The only way to do this is to make the movement with your shoulders, back, and chest. If the shafts aren't moving at the same speed, your wrists are overactive and creating inconsistencies in your putting stroke. This is one of my favorite drills—I created it with my producer Kevin Schultz on the set of *The Golf Fix*.

Wrapping Paper

PROBLEM: Gripping the club too tightly

PURPOSE: Teaches you how to have consistent grip pressure

PROCEDURE: Take a piece of 8½" x 11" paper. You know what I'm talking about—the paper you used to write too many compositions in school. Wrap the grip with the paper. Then take your grip, and try to make sure that you don't make any noise with the paper while making your stroke. If you hear the paper at any time, you're changing your grip pressure. Changes in grip pressure can have so many bad effects on a putt, and the primary one is on the tempo of the stroke. And you know what poor tempo can do to your distance control.

4. FACE

Two for One

PROBLEM: Difficulty making contact with a square face

PURPOSE: Make sure the heel and toe are moving at the same speed

PROCEDURE: The proper way to hit a putt is with the toe and heel of the club moving through the impact zone at the same time. But golfers frequently hit the ball with either the toe or the heel of the putter leading the way, causing the face of the putter to be either open or closed. That will cause a change in intended direction or create an undesired sidespin. So how do you work on eliminating that? Place two golf balls on the green perpendicular to the hole. One will be what I call a toe ball, and the other a heel ball. Set the putter up so that the toe and heel are equidistant from the toe ball and heel ball. The goal is to contact both balls at the same time, and believe me—it's easier said than done. When you first perform the drill, you'll likely see the heel ball leave the putter before the toe ball, and it will probably go farther. That's because the face is open at impact. Work on this drill until you can make either both golf balls leave the putter at the same time, *or* the toe ball go first. There's a reason why having the toe ball go first is OK—it means that the face has released and the ball will have a topspin. And as I've said many times throughout the book, topspin is the desired spin. I'm looking for the kind of contact with the ball that will create topspin, and this drill will help with that.

Heel ball first

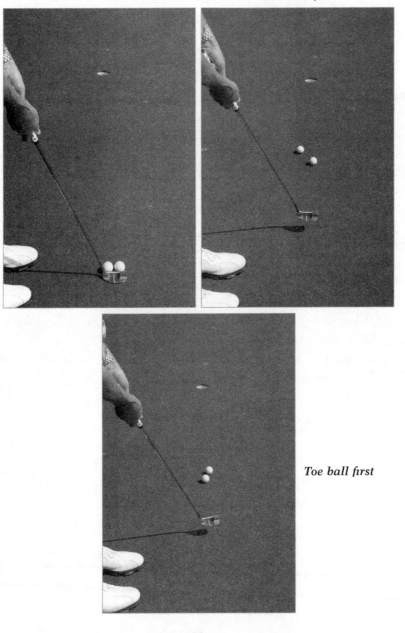

Toe ball first

Wooden Dowel

PROBLEM: Inconsistent contact with the putter

PURPOSE: Improve your impact position

PROCEDURE: This is another great drill for controlling the putterface. It's very challenging to perform well, but once you get proficient at it, you'll have great control over the face. And it's very simple to understand. Lay a dowel on the ground on the target line and parallel to the line. The dowel should be about six to eight inches long and a half-inch or so in diameter. Make a putting stroke and hit the dowel so that it slides on the ground along the target line and maintains its parallel relationship. If the dowel spins off the putterhead in a clockwise fashion, the putterface was facing to the right when contact occurred. If the dowel spins off the putterhead in a counterclockwise fashion, the putterface was facing to the left. The purpose is to become consistent with your impact point on the golf ball. When you get consistent with your impact point, you'll be consistent with the face of the club and ultimately much better with your distance control. This drill can also be performed with an AA battery. It's much more challenging with the battery, but just as effective.

Field Goal

PROBLEM: Difficulty starting the putt on the intended line

PURPOSE: Focus on the initial direction of the putt

PROCEDURE: We often miss putts because of an inability to start the ball where we want—that is, on the desired line. There are a number of reasons for this. I always look at what the face is doing when I'm struggling with that part of my game, because the face can be too open or too closed. An inability to start the ball on the desired line can also occur when too much loft is added during the stroke. Another reason is as simple as poor aim. Regardless of the reason, this drill will help improve the problem. Place two tees 3 inches apart and 1 foot in front of the golf ball. Start with a 3-foot putt, and make sure the putt is straight. Hit the putt through the field goal—that is, between the two tees. If you're having trouble getting the ball started on line, there's no need to put break into the putt. You should be able to make ten putts in a row from this distance without hitting the tees in front of you. Once you're able to do this, move back to 6 feet. As your ability to perform the drill on straight putts improves, move to breaking putts. I would suggest that when you start adding break, start with putts that break off the edge of the hole, and again I'd begin with 6-foot putts (because it's hard to find a putt that breaks much from a distance of three feet). Make sure to hit putts that break right to left and left to right. By hitting putts that break both ways, you'll get comfortable with all breaking putts. I cannot emphasize this enough. You must develop confidence with putts of all kinds of break, and if you practice both breaks, you'll develop that.

5. PATH

Alignment Rails

PROBLEM: Trouble with consistent putter and golf ball path

PURPOSE: Get the putter and ball to travel down the line toward the target

PROCEDURE: Take two alignment rods—or if those are not available, use a pair of golf clubs, preferably a 5- and 6-iron—and lay them on the ground parallel to each other. Make sure that they're about 5 or 6 inches apart with the heads of the clubs closer to the target and turned toward the outside of the channel they're creating. They should be on the ground so that the center of the channel is directly in line with the intended target. The way you do this is to first put an alignment rod on the ground headed at your intended target. Then place the other two alignment rods on the ground equidistant from the alignment rod used for the target. Once you have the rods lined up properly, put the golf ball into the channel where the grips are. Begin with a 3-foot putt, because the stroke you make for a putt of that length is small, and you'll see quite easily what the putter is doing. Also, it'll be much easier to line the channel up correctly when you first perform the drill from 3 feet. After a number of practice sessions, you'll be comfortable enough to start at whatever length putt you feel you need to practice. I would also urge you to practice both right-to-left and left-to-right breaking putts, The other thing I like about this drill is that it *may* (emphasis on *may*) help you to visualize a path to the target. It doesn't do this for everyone, because as I mentioned earlier in the book, some players see paths or lines when they putt and others don't. Those who see lines *may* benefit from this in that regard.

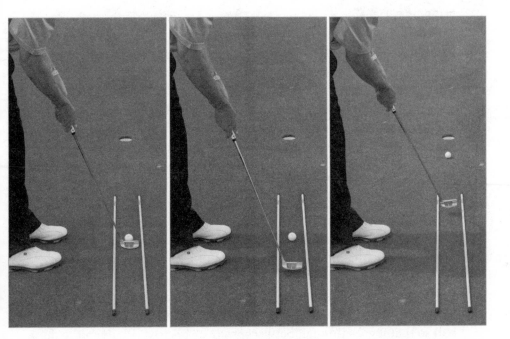

The Putting Scope

PROBLEM: Putter path and golf ball aren't following the intended target line

PURPOSE: Develop good alignment and a consistent putter path

PROCEDURE: This will require a little bit of work on your part, and some cash. But it's well worth the investment. You'll need to purchase a device that I invented called the Putting Scope. You can find it at eye linegolf.com. It's simply the best putting instructional device out there, and it's very easy to use. Furthermore, it makes putting practice great fun.

Begin by finding a straight putt about 3 feet in length. Place the Putting Scope on the ground so that it's aligned toward your intended target. Place the ball under the alignment rod in the center of the device and putt the ball through the scope (1). Because the opening in the Putting Scope is smaller than the hole, both the putter path and putterface must be perfectly aligned with the target in order to make the ball go through the scope. Once you've become comfortable with the three-footers, lengthen the putts to 5 feet. Once you've become proficient with the five-footer, place the ball outside the scope and putt the ball so that it goes through both scopes (2). This is very difficult to do, however—if you can do this three times in a row, you will have become a Zen master! Just kidding, but it really will help improve your putting dramatically. It's pretty difficult, but it's extremely good for your focus and your putting stroke. The Putting Scope is also a great way to learn proper alignment. When you position the scope on the green, you know exactly where you're aiming, regardless of where it may feel like you're aiming. When one of my students is struggling with his alignment, I have him use the Putting Scope every day for two weeks! Poor putting strokes are so often a result of poor alignment, and this drill will correct that issue.

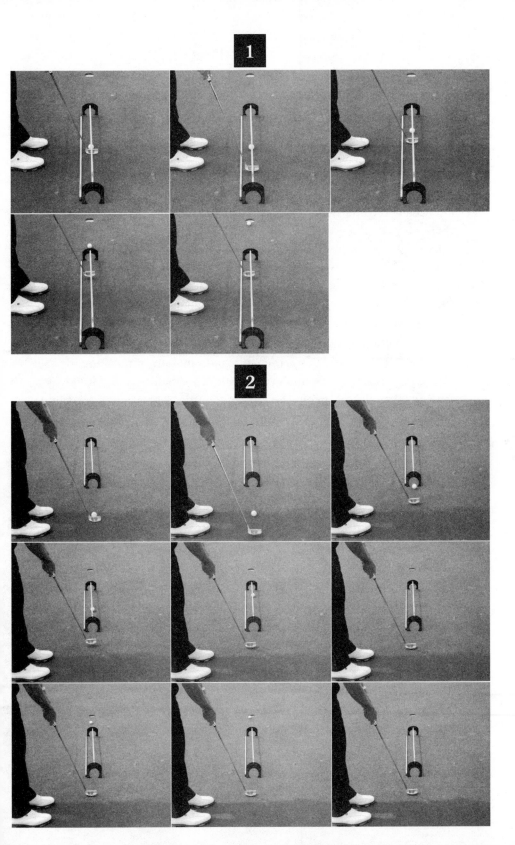

Toilet Paper

PROBLEM: Difficulty with putter path and ball path

PURPOSE: Develop good alignment and a consistent putter path

PROCEDURE: You need a roll of toilet paper. Roll the TP out so that there's a path along the ground about 5 feet long. Put a golf ball in the middle of the path and hit putts toward the leg of a chair or some other object—you can even rig up a makeshift golf hole using a plastic cup from the cupboard (a glass, however, is probably a bad idea . . .). The goal is to work on alignment and a consistent ball path, but the drill may also help with visualization. It may sound funny, but some golfers—including many of my students—find that after practicing with the TP, they start to see the white path in their mind when they're on the putting green. So don't rule it out. This drill is great for keeping your putting sharp during the winter months, when you're traveling, or during inclement weather.

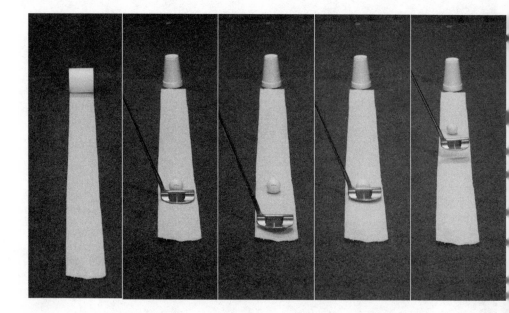

6. SPEED/DISTANCE CONTROL

Pace Maker

PROBLEM: Poor distance control

PURPOSE: Develop the correct sense of speed

PROCEDURE: My first and still favorite drill is one that teaches you how to putt for pace, and I recommend you do it every time you go to the course. Place two tees about 2 feet apart, so they look like goalposts in an end zone, and stand 10 feet away. Drop three balls on the green. I want you to use three because 1) that's the number of golf balls in a sleeve, and 2) once is luck, twice is coincidence, and three times is consistency. The goal of the drill is to hit the balls and get them to stop on the line. Be concerned with the dispersion between the closest and farthest balls. From 10 feet, you should end up with no more than 6 inches between the three balls. When you get proficient at that distance, go back, to 15 feet, then 20, and then 25. This is very effective when you're getting ready to play a course that you don't know, because it will enable you to discern the speed of the greens.

Knock-Nudge Drill

PROBLEM: Inability to control speed

PURPOSE: Teach yourself how to attain desired pace

PROCEDURE: Place two golf balls on flat ground about three feet apart. Putt one ball so it makes contact with the other. Now here's the hard part: You must vary your speed with each stroke. Use the "knock" speed to putt the first ball hard enough to make it collide with the other ball. Then impart the "nudge" speed so that the ball you're putting barely touches the second one. To get good at this drill from 3 feet requires some practice. But once you've mastered that distance, go back to 6 feet and then 9. You'll soon find that your distance control from all of these distances is excellent. I know because I've done this drill with my students thousands of times, and I've never had one of them leave a putt short from 6 feet. Not even once!

Push Ball

PROBLEM: Decelerating into the hit

PURPOSE: Learn to follow through to the target

PROCEDURE: This is a great drill if you're having trouble with deceleration. Rest the putterface against the ball and then simply push the ball to the target. Don't make any backswing. Start with 3-foot putts, and then move to six- and nine-footers. I wouldn't go past 9 feet, because hitting putts that way from longer distances will begin to create too much wrist activity. And too much wristiness, as I'm sure you know by now, will keep you from becoming a consistent putter.

7. GAMES

Blocking the Hole

PROBLEM: Inconsistent speed on breaking putts

PURPOSE: See the entry point of the ball into the hole

PROCEDURE: This is another speed drill, but now you're introducing the hole. It's also one that you should do every time you step onto a practice putting green. This drill requires a tee. Place the tee in the ground so that it blocks the low side of the hole. The first putt you hit should be from 6 feet and have about 3 inches of hook break. By that I mean a right-to-left break for right-handed putters and a left-to-right break for left-handed putters. When you block part of the hole, you obviously make the hole smaller, and anytime you make the hole smaller, you're forcing yourself to concentrate on both speed and line. Perform this drill from 6 feet and hit ten putts in a row on right-to-left-breaking putts. After you've made ten in a row, do the same on left-to-right-breaking putts. Typically, if you go to the opposite side of the hole, you'll find the same amount of break in the opposite direction. When you get to where you can make ten in a row from 6 feet on both right-to-left and left-to-right breaks, extend the putt to 9, 12, and then 15 feet. It will take some time to master this drill, so be patient. But once you get to a point where you're making fifteen-footers with part of the hole being blocked, you're well on your way to becoming a great putter. You'll see your ability to read greens improve, too.

Ten

PROBLEM: Difficulty making important short putts

PURPOSE: Make ten putts in a row

PROCEDURE: Take three golf balls and position yourself initially 3 feet from the hole. Begin by hitting dead-straight putts. Your goal is to make ten in a row from 3 feet. Once you've made ten in a row from that distance over five straight practice sessions, progress to breaking putts. Make sure to hit putts with both left-to-right and right-to-left breaks. Once you've made those, move to 4 feet. At each distance you should be hitting three types of putts: straight, left-to-right, and right-to-left. The goal is to get to the point where you're consistently knocking in putts from 10 feet.

Around the World

PROBLEM: Difficulty making important short putts

PURPOSE: Learn to putt successfully with pressure

PROCEDURE: This is a very important drill to perform every practice session, because you're going to have to make important 3- to 6-foot putts in every round. There is a self-induced pressure that occurs when you stand over a "must-make" putt. Yet we rarely practice them. No longer! Take four golf balls. Place them at each of the four compass points around the cup (north, south, east, and west) about 3 feet from the hole. The idea is to make all four putts in a row. By placing the balls at each of these four points around the hole, you're ensuring that you'll have to practice right-to-left, left-to-right, uphill, and downhill putts. After you've made all four in a row, move to six-footers. When you've made all four in a row from this distance, move on to nine-footers. Finally, make all four 9-foot putts in a row. If you make all of the three- and six-footers but miss the first 9-foot putt, start back at the 3-foot putts. When you're able to make all twelve in a row, you will have become a great putter from 9 feet and closer.

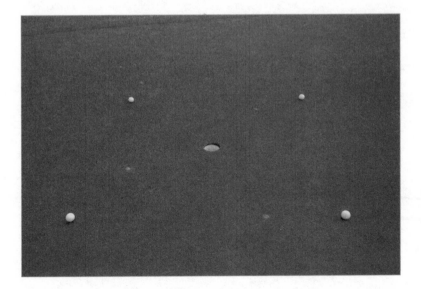

Ladder Drill

PROBLEM: You struggle to make important putts

PURPOSE: To teach yourself to make important putts

PROCEDURE: There are five different-length putts in this drill—3, 6, 9, 12, and 15 feet. Start with the three-footer. When you make that, move back to 6 feet, then to 9 feet, and so forth. If you miss along the way, go back to the previous distance. You're hitting one putt from each length and moving to a longer or shorter putt depending on the make or miss. This is another drill that you should perform from four sides of the hole to get putts with different breaks and speeds. Do it by yourself, or with a friend.

20-Point Must

PROBLEM: Difficulty making important putts

PURPOSE: Make putts to earn at least 20 points

PROCEDURE: This is a great game to play either alone or with a friend. You're going to hit putts from 3 feet, 9 feet, 15 feet, and 21 feet from the four sides of each hole. The point system works as follows: making a 3-foot putt is worth one point, a nine-footer two points, a 15-foot putt three points, and a 21-foot putt four points. If you miss the 3-foot putt, you lose 3 points. If you miss any of the other putts, you don't lose any points unless the golf ball stops outside of the safety zone, which is a 2-foot area from the front of the cup to 2 feet behind the hole. You're trying to accumulate at least 20 points, and the first player to get there wins the game. You must finish the lap of the four spots around the hole even if you get to 20 points, because you can still lose points if your golf ball stops outside the safety zone. If you're playing against a friend, you should alternate laps, but each player hits all four putts in a row from each side, beginning with a three-footer and moving up to 21 feet. Should a player make all four putts on a given lap in a row, he continues his turn. You should initially choose a putt that is straight and uphill. When you've reached the 20-point goal, switch to a right-to-left putt. Make sure to hit putts from four sides of the hole so you get to hit both types of breaks and uphill and downhill putts. You'll quickly discover which types of putts you're comfortable with and which putts you need to practice. I like this drill so much that I have all of my touring professionals using it. I got it from Todd Sones, who is a friend and a very well-respected instructor. He definitely has a winner with this one.

ACKNOWLEDGMENTS

Michael Breed Acknowledgments

My mother, Rebecca . . . Your guidance, leadership, wisdom, and grace are only a few of the many qualities I have admired for my life. I love you very much and couldn't have been more fortunate to have parents like you and Pop!

Giff, Alan, and Becky . . . There is nothing I can say. I love you all and am so proud to be your brother.

Betsy Grob . . . I could never have done this without you. Your friendship has always been most important.

Mark Reiter . . . Amazing what a lunch can do. Thanks for your vision.

John Steinbreder . . . Thanks for your tireless work and insight. It is amazing we did this!

Ray Corcoran . . . Cup, you are the best!

Sunningdale Country Club . . . I am grateful for being your head golf professional. Thank you for your trust in me.

Tom S. and Tony T. . . . Thank you for believing in me. What a gift you have given me.

Schultzy, Hentch, Rut, Juice, Bret . . . Mondays have never been so fun. Thanks for all of your hard work and creativity.

Ted K., Hendy, Darrell, and Doc K. . . . Thanks for your guidance and friendship.

Craig, Paul, and St. Andrews Club . . . Thanks for your gracious hospitality. What a beautiful club you have. I know you're all very proud.

Lou . . . The pictures look great. Thanks for your professionalism.

I would also like to offer a special thanks to those at the Acushnet Company: Wally, Peter, Steve, Antoinette, Jay, Cheryl, Mary Lou, and all of those who have provided the best products possible. I can't thank you enough for your support.

Bill Shinker and Travers Johnson from Gotham Books who believed in the idea and were overly patient with my schedule. Thank you!

John Steinbreder Acknowledgments

Thanks to my wife, the lovely Cynthia, for making each day we spend together pure joy.

Thanks, also, to my daughters, Exa and Lydia, for the love they shower on us and the pleasure they bring. We could not be luckier.

Mom, you are the best. I only wish we lived closer together.

Here's to my sisters, Sissy, Gillett and Sarah, who I miss as much as I love, and to my in-laws, Pat and Tom, as well as Kendall, Stephen, Tucker, and Karen. How lucky am I to have two great families!

Breeder, you are the best, with as keen an eye for the written word as for the golf swing. You made this book better than I could have ever imagined, and I appreciate all your time and effort.

Kerri, I am thankful to have met you, and delighted you and Michael have found each other.

I am also grateful to Mark Reiter for his help and vision, as well as his friendship. It's great to be working together again. A doff of the golf visor to Bill Shinker and Travers Johnson from Gotham Books, too, for all their support and assistance.

As Michael is a head-to-toe Acushnet guy, I am reminded of my many friendships at that company and want to express my gratitude to Wally Uihlein, Joe Gomes, George Sine, Mary Lou Bohn, Peter Broome, Jeff Harmet, Joe Nauman, Scotty Cameron, Chris McGinley, Jim Connor, Andy Jones, and Rob Kelley. You make great equipment, you care so much about the game, and you take great care of me. Thanks for that.

Finally, my heartfelt appreciation to Jim Nugent and my colleagues at *Global Golf Post* for such a great writing gig.

Truly, my cup runneth over.

ABOUT THE AUTHORS

Michael Breed is one of the top teaching professionals in golf today. He is the host of *The Golf Fix*, which is seen on the Golf Channel by one million viewers in more than seventy countries each week, and the PGA Head Professional at the Sunningdale Country Club in Scarsdale, New York. Breed is also a regular contributor to *Golf Magazine,* where he is ranked as one of the top hundred golf instructors in the United States, and he is a two-time winner of the Metropolitan PGA Teacher of the Year award. A former assistant professional at Augusta National Golf Club, Breed has instructed a number of PGA and LPGA touring pros, among them Darron Stiles, Ron Whittaker, Shaun Michael, Joe Ogilvie, and Meaghan Francella.

John Steinbreder is a senior correspondent for *Global Golf Post*, a columnist and feature writer for Masters.com, and the author of twelve books. He has reported on the game from five continents and received nine honors for his work from the Golf Writers Association of America, and nine from the International Network of Golf.